# Shadows of The Soul

*. . . a book half written*

N.E.C. Iankowitz

AuthorHouse™
1663 Liberty Drive
Bloomington, IN 47403
www.authorhouse.com
Phone: 833-262-8899

This book is printed on acid-free paper.

ISBN: 978-1-6655-2267-0 (sc)
ISBN: 978-1-6655-2268-7 (e)

Library of Congress Control Number: 2021907558

Print information available on the last page.

Published by AuthorHouse  11/29/2021

author**HOUSE**

# Other Books by This Author

Marcy and Her Friends
Conversations with Our Daughters
Tales of The Soil

# Other Articles & Essays by This Author

Feeding Positive Energy Throughout the COVID-19 Holiday Season
Hunkering Down During COVID-19
The Stress and Strain of COVID-19 on Relationships
Parenthood: a Continuing Journey
Finding Your Joy
The Mind, Body, and Spirit Approach to Self-Care
The Deep Dive for Love
Second Childhood - The Intangible Spirit
How Your Hobby May Heal You
Holiday Health and Wellness
Relationship Gone Sour: Parents and Adult Children (Getting Back on Track)
Building Lasting Relationships
Protecting Our Children from Our Anxiety
Congestive Heart Failure: A Functional Medicine Approach
Lifestyle Tools That Become Lifelong Lifesaving Gifts
Caring For Aging Parents
Refilling the Empty Nest with Dignity and Grace
When the Foods You Love Don't Love You Back
You Are Probably Dehydrated If . . .
Safety in the Summer Sun

# Table of Contents

# Preface

The human condition, from birth to death, sings its melody at each transition. Snapshots of that passage are what we call art, poetry, music. Those able to capture such moments are the gifted few, from whom we may learn about that which we are, and where we have been.

This book is of that journey. It speaks to the soul. Woven throughout the poems, posters, and short stories are whispers of truth too often missed along life's adventure.

With respect,

Dr. L. Nehoc, Author *Illusion:Redefined*

# Foreword

Healing through grief is the focus of much of this collection. The reader will discover essences and truths interwoven throughout pages which, though intended to stand on their own, harmonize with each other – much like instruments in an orchestra or voices in a choir. You are the conductor of this metaphoric vibration. From my perspective, any creative process delivers only inspiration – offered by the writer, musician, artist, dancer, etc., leaving fulfillment of the offering's potential to the observer; thus, it is up to each reader to complete this book.

Skip among the chapters and view all through your own unique lens. *Shadows of The Soul* is intended to bring comfort and peace of mind through validation. Veracity resonates within the imagination, embraced or rejected in response to our position along our healing adventure. Life, for some, is a self-editing process. Personal growth welcomes that which facilitates our highest self, and releases what no longer serves us. It is my hope that this book nourishes your soul.

As spirits traveling a sacred path on earth, we are never alone. At times, threads on this side of life's tapestry seem haphazard, loose, dark, illogical, and even 'unfair' – but the marvelous work of art, of which we are all an intricate part, can become an exciting portal of joy, enlightenment, and satisfaction.

I'm deeply grateful for your time and interest, and invite you to complete this book on pages provided. If you are so inclined, please share your thoughts and interpretations with me directly, as I'm eager to see this book made whole through your eyes. My personal email: neciankowitz@yahoo.com (write *"Shadows of The Soul"* in the subject line).

Namaste,

*N.E.C. Iankowitz* DNP, RN, FNP-BC
Family Nurse Practitioner
Holistic and Integrative Healing LLC, Director

# On Love

Love inspires goodness – the best version of yourself;
truth-to-spirit, honesty – not trophies on a shelf.

Love is not pretend – it fills the heart, the mind, the soul.
Loving is connecting – not performing just for show.

Love pays close attention; offers empathy and care.
Love can buffer tragedy and soften deep despair.

Love is safety, peace of mind – pure trust and loyalty.
Love beams forth from inner light – a force that all can see.

True love isn't selfish – it is generous and kind.
Love is clear sweet clarity – not envious or blind.

Honest love feeds gratitude of heart, of soul, of mind.
Love that's true is rare – a gift that precious few can find.

If you've ever found forever in another's eyes,
     guard it and protect it for its G-d's most fragile prize.

Love is meant to channel goodness – hopeful energy. . .
Love that is authentic heals and sets two spirits free.

Inspirational

# When

When the days you wonder if you should get out of bed
      are met by you with courage, and you face the world instead;
          though inner dialogue that cuts you down streams through your head,
             you take charge of each new step turning lights to green from red . . .

When the days that threaten joy can't overtake your mood . . .
When you keep perspective though you're blamed by those who brood . . .
When you hold yourself to standards higher than the rest;
      regardless of who's watching, you still do your very best . . .
When the words of others who spew hatred don't offend . . .
When you trust your heart to see through 'fake' in a false friend . . .
When you can stay focused and avoid toxic intrusions
      of others who insist you honor their self-taught delusions . . .
When you have the strength to live your truth, eyes open wide . . .
When you can be your best friend without a need to hide . . .

When you can be generous, yet keep some for yourself . . .
When you give and know when to put 'giving' on the shelf . . .
When your guide is honesty; you look *you* in the eye . . .
When you have the courage to dissolve each self-taught lie . . .

When you disagree with someone who's dear to your heart,
      and fairly self-reflect, whether together or apart . . .
When you pay each blessing forward and don't advertise . . .
When you listen closely and don't gossip or advise . . .
When you know your value yet stay humble as a friend,
      and self-respect and trust define your truth without pretend . . .

When your heart is open chakra, giving, and you care . . .
When you're cautious – just enough, yet strong enough to dare . . .

When you can be 'present' even when you walk away . . .
When you have the courage to trust 'vibes' through what 'they say'. . .
When you're not 'entitled' but still know what you deserve,
     and temper your emotions clinging to that last raw nerve . . .
When you can accept you are 'just human' and can say:
*"I am seeking truth to self"* you've reached that perfect day.

When you know you 'need' and yet you're brave enough to give,
     you will taste the Universe - and life is yours to live.
When those days of confidence that fill you with deep pride
     are days you can embrace the awesome feeling deep inside
        without a need to post the news on Facebook –
           you've arrived.

*Your thoughts*

# The Visits Are Just Right

Grandma I know you miss PopPop. We all miss him too.
Here's a picture of that time we all went to the zoo.
I loved how he held your hand, and how his eyes would smile
   every time you'd say, "One moment" but took such a while
     to make sure every hair in place was perfect just for him.
Then you would walk over and he'd gently touch your chin.

I loved how you held his face so sweetly in your hands
   nodding 'no' while loving eyes said, "I don't understand!"
     each time that he made those jokes and said such silly things.
After 50 years your vows renewed with brand new rings.

Grandma do you hear me? I am sitting next to you.
Grandma are you crying 'cause of all that you've been through?
Do you see the photo here? Am I upsetting you?
When your tears roll down your face, I don't know what to do.

*Child, I wish you understood my mind and words don't meet.*
*I wish I could tell you now, I'm grateful and complete.*
*Yes, I know the stories you remember and you tell.*
*I recall the photos and the memories so well.*
*Though I can't put words to this, I hope my eyes convey*
   *that I'm feeling blessed that you are by my side today.*
*I do miss your PopPop but in my dreams every night*
   *we are both together and the visits are just right.*
*Sometimes my words slip by day; you hear me talk to him.*
*That's my vision clearing as the tapestry grows thin.*
*Soon I'll join your PopPop and I hope you'll always know,*
   *we are both so proud of you and how you choose to grow.*

*Stay true to your spirit; let your wisdom light the way.*
*Nourish healing energy – don't follow those who stray.*

*Deep breaths when you're anxious; know you're worthy, strong, and kind.*
*Pick your battles carefully, when you do you will find*
*goodness lives in many, though sometimes it seems to hide.*
*Gift yourself 'forgiveness' keeping your eyes open wide.*
*When betrayed, draw boundaries; when you can, just 'let it slide' . . .*
*Channel pure sweet energy as long as you're alive.*

*Your thoughts*

# Strength to Let Go (Life's Two-Wheeler)

I saw you, because you let me.
You were right there by my side, until you let go.
You didn't tell me, and I didn't look back,
      until I was too far out of your reach.
I was thrilled. I was furious.
I trusted you. I felt you let me down.
It took just a moment to go from a trike to a two-wheeler,
      but all of these years to understand, and let go of the anger . . .
        of the confused jumble of mixed feelings which made me
          so independent – so furious.
It took until today, when it became my turn.

Time removed her training wheels.
She was excited and nervous. I had faith she would succeed.
She pleaded with me to not let her fall. I promised I'd be there for her.
She saw me, because I let her.
She was confident because she knew I was there.
I helped her keep her balance until I felt she was ready.
I let go for one, then two seconds –
      yet, once she became unsteady,
        I felt my fingers tighten under her seat.
It took great effort, but I managed to loosen my grip – ever so slightly,
      once she began to fall.
She tried to steady herself with fury in her eyes,
      . . . and I saw me yelling at you "for letting go".

If I had truly 'let go', my wrist wouldn't be so twisted and sore.
I controlled her fall because I needed to help her anticipate the motion.
Now what I need is to learn how to let her ride out of my reach.
I still feel the need to buffer her falls.

It will take much courage and confidence in all I've given to her over the years . . .
A great deal of inner strength for me to permit her to test herself.

I knew she'd be angry.
Maybe she will stay angry deep inside,
        until after she has the pleasure of helping her first child
            learn to ride life's two-wheeler.

I look forward to the moment
        her fury becomes respect and admiration,
            as did mine.
More importantly, I wish her the wonderful satisfaction of exploring
        her incredible personal strength . . . and the awesome enlightenment
            which comes only from discovery of her honest feelings.
I wish her, too, inner tranquility born of the ability to "let go"
        of all inevitable misunderstandings natural in the mind of a child.

I know I will continue to be here for her, unconditionally,
        as you have always been for me.
All I will need is to find and grasp the power
        I now know was within your reach,
            so that I might finally and truly let her ride "too far" out of mine.

*Your thoughts*

# Leaving Toyland Behind

In adolescence and early adulthood, most bang their heads through bumpy relationships filled with self-defensive postures, hurt feelings, and confusion.

As we mature, competition with others is replaced by competition within the self; the goal: to become our own best version each new day. Envy of others is replaced by joy for their success; we learn to discover and embrace worthy mentors so we, too, might contribute positive energy to the world around us – unencumbered by distraction.

Win/lose arguments are traded for win/win scenarios wherein both celebrate victory at establishment of common ground. Communication is mutual rather than combative. Explanations are offered to dissolve tension rather than to button push, irritate, or otherwise deflect a spotlight off our own poor choices.

Healthy adulthood facilitates recognition that

- self-reflection is a super power to be embraced not feared
- sometimes, people react to external events having nothing to do with us
- when baffled by a trusted friend, clarification eases strain through understanding
- gifts of self-care and forgiveness begin within the spirit
- generosity doesn't flow from an empty bucket
- strength of character offers empathy, refusing to absorb the festering pain of others
- the wise don't jump to conclusions or accept responsibility for others' false assumptions

# Growing Pains

Limit testing, button pushing - oh, it's all so clear!
Teens and adolescents self-define this way for years.
Drives most parents crazy, and the siblings all go nuts.
Tweens feign deep confusion by "unnecessary fuss."

Facts are facts – throughout these 'growing pains' it's sad, but true:
    self-esteem, though craved by all, accomplished by too few.
When it's safe at home, the personality can shift . . .
    attitudes adopted that may cause a family rift
        find their way to compromise – a rare and precious gift.
Wisdom offers boundaries, and acceptance helps kids grow . . .
    free to taste their options when the parents can let go.
Teens tear through their chrysalis to test unfolding wings.
They compose their spirit song – unique for them to sing.

Toyland lacking harmony steals gifts of notes and song.
Silence fuels rejection by the silenced – if they're strong.
Toddlers who are not encouraged to share hopes and fears
    stumble through adulthood choosing misery and tears.
Toyland is for questioning; the sounding board is: home.
Questions not permitted fester; healthy love: unknown.
Empty eyes lack empathy; the frightened can't reflect.
Distance masks the self that needs to hide so none detect.
Like limp legs, sad hearts ignore the sweetness of life's dance.
Only once potential is fulfilled can one dare chance.
If, by luck, a soulmate is discovered – there's a flame.
Love and joy, reserved for those true to their Spirit name.

# A Mother's Wish for Her Daughter

Have self-respect.
Take pride in fulfillment of your potential.
Embrace those who gravitate towards you for who you are; they help nourish your
highest self. Avoid people who seek you out only because of their perception of what
you can do for them; they will manipulate, con, abuse, and ultimately hurt you.
Invest in those deserving of your energy. If you discover one is unworthy, set boundaries.
The earnest will be honored to be in your presence, manufacturing time to share
because you are deep, courageous, honest, caring, and filled with love.
Trust yourself and those who pass your litmus tests - those vibrations that inform; instincts.
Remain true to your inner spirit; avoid self-distraction and all who encourage it,
as they put energy into avoidance of fulfilling their own potential.
Permit caution and logic to guide when those you once trusted attempt to pressure you;
find strength to redefine safe healthy boundaries and move on.
Respect your body enough to not pollute it.
Respect your mind enough to not try to 'fool' it.

You have wisdom, courage, and strength to make decisions you can be proud of. Cut yourself
slack when appropriate. Try to resist the temptation to test life's unforgiving limits; select your
paths by 'regrets' you are willing to live with. Once inevitable mistakes are revealed, tap into
maturity to look yourself straight in the eye and correct what you can; then, forgive yourself and
move to a higher plain of existence. I am so proud of the young woman you are becoming.

# New Love

If we met last year, you would have looked the other way.
I had not arrived to be who stands so tall today.
Learning of this path through life - one I could take with you,
seems to be a dream - I want to jump into the view.
Feels as if the path I walked alone was dark and cold.
Now, with you, excitement with each step seems to unfold.
Suddenly I understand potential to fulfill.
In your eyes I see all I can be - I can and will.

## Your thoughts

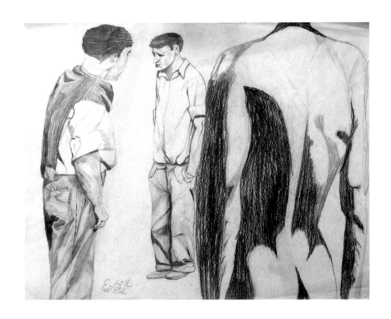

# Battle for Your Soul

Once you know just who you are and learn your Spirit Name,
  paths will open. You will walk without guilt, fear, or shame.
Understand your essence and embrace the light that shines
    within your soul – a gift to all, and our job to remind
        each and every person who we meet all journey long:
            they, too, have that light that shines.
  It guides us to be strong.
Next time your reflection shows the truth inside of you,
  view the imperfections using courage, strong and true.
Only once you see the errors can you make them right.
  Fortitude and self-respect: tools; for your soul you fight.

## Acceptance

Fish cannot explain their life to birds or butterflies.
Snakes shed skin and turtles keep their shell for when they're shy.
Trees reach up while roots dig down – no creature wonders why
the Pond reflects the Sun & moonlit stars that dress the sky.
As with Creatures of The Meadow – we all live and grow,
repeating generations with each seed we're blessed to sow.

## Second Chance

I was shocked each time you said: "Just FIX it!" I was weak.
Only knew to run in fear – my life was 'hide and seek'.
Wasn't just a game for me, it's what my parents taught.
Then we met. It's clear now . . . into many lies I bought.
I avoided mirrors. I refused to self-reflect.
Just knew how to con, gaslight, hide from myself, deflect . . .
Freaks me out to think of all I put our children through.
So ashamed of how I stressed the life I forced on you.
It's been painful, and I know the pain was caused by me.
Failed us both by shirking my responsibility.

I must answer inner dialogue that cuts me down.
I can handle this with power – I'll turn this around!
I will rise above distractions of my toxic past.
My goal: honestly invest to feed love that can last.

If you find it in your spirit to accept this plea,
I swear to be true to us . . . replacing "I" with "we".

If there's still a chance for "us" – if your heart hasn't gone . . .
I vow to match words with actions from this moment on.

Realizing I broke trust – there's much for me to earn.
Please don't answer - not until I prove all I have learned.

*Your thoughts*

## I Am Enough

When trapped in the Ocean drop, no mercy – just despair.
Thought I'd never have a voice . . . if I did – who would care?
Suddenly, evaporation – what a lovely view.
Part of something so majestic – I was every hue.
Drifted to an island on a fluffy, friendly cloud.
Claps of thunder. Bolts of lightning. Forced to join the crowd.
Racing to the island I lamented what would be.
Struggled to define myself – had no identity.
Was I snowflake? Ocean? Rainbow? Was I morning dew?
Did I have a purpose after all that I'd been through?
Then the answer soothed my soul. My job: facilitate.
I learned how to float, quench, carve, decay, and help create.
Just by being what I am, I heal more than I see.
Lesson learned. I am 'enough' – that's all that I can be.

# The Bitter Taste of Distraction

The lens through which we view our past, if tainted by regret,
        may trigger an awakening for growth - the first small step.
If distracted by imposters: 'guilt', 'shame', 'blame' just three . . .
        truth is masked; we're blinded to what centered eyes might see.
If distracted, fact is: we're not all that we can be.
Focus on 'distraction' for a moment and you'll see
        it is really nothing more than opportunity.
Each response to invitations that require your action
        offers choices: to succeed or fail (from self-distraction).

Ask self: have I felt regret? Do I step up to act?
Do I hide from truth? Do I permit shame to distract?
Do I blame another for decisions that I made?
Do I beat my Spirit up for actions I displayed?

If you ask these questions, know the answers won't be clear
        if soiled by agenda 'to avoid' – or, if there's 'fear'.
Fear's the next distraction from essential self-reflection.
It takes strength to ask and honestly address each question.
I wish you, the reader this: *your* true awakening.
Once you self-reflect, you'll answer each and everything.
Often Universe extends such gentle invitations;
        if they're missed, they then become loud, outright declarations.

Once awake, the Spirit knows when it has been betrayed.
Courage clarifies through recognition: "I've been played."
Step up to life's plate with bat in hand – growth has begun . . .
        a benched soul forfeits any chance to swing and score a run.

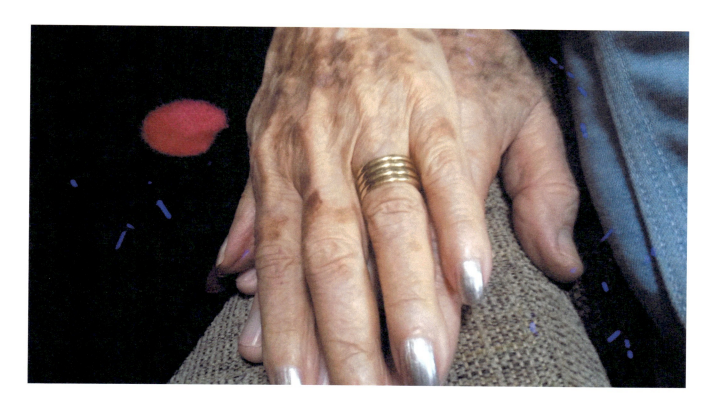

## 51 Years In Love

You are my inspiration . . . my guiding lights . . .
Setting examples for marriage, relationships, parenting, living, learning, growing,
taking care of one's self and one's partner.
You are always there for each other, continuing to encourage mutual growth and yet,
you remain patient with each other in a most extraordinary way.
Time has nurtured a kind of forgiveness, wisdom, compassion, and understanding
that I can only begin to imagine and hope to, one day, truly fathom.
You encourage your children to look deeply into themselves to resolve issues,
even if those insights illuminate what might painfully point to you guys
and the minor mistakes you might have made as young parents/grandparents.

You are the strongest most unselfish people I know.

You are gentle, caring, supportive, and always there for your children. In many ways your life rhythm does not match mine; nonetheless, you found it within yourselves to instill in me the confidence to stand on my own, and the comfort to know you are there beside me.

I can't imagine life without you, but I know that I don't have to worry about that, because time and the universe will take care of these concerns. I recall fearing that I'd never be able to tuck myself in at night . . . second grade was a companion fear at that time.

You are the best role models one could hope to have for a successful, loving marital relationship. I love and respect you guys, and I thank the universal energy for all it delivers to me through you. I remain so grateful that you are the parents to whom I was given, and the married couple I can look to as an example.

Happy Anniversary and here's to many more in love and good health.

*In celebration of the 51st wedding anniversary of Nita and Dan Cohen 2/9/2008*

*Your thoughts*

From the
Other Side of
The Rainbow

# Journey

Eyelids stained as if tattooed, she sees what is not there.
He adores her as he strokes her head and soft gray hair.
Years of sunshine so enjoyed have marked her fragile skin.
Wisdom she was known for now floats in and out again.

Her life was so full; embraced her matriarchal role . . .
      thus, witnessing transition such as this does take a toll.
Now I'm here for both of them as they have been for me . . .
      not because "I should" - because it's where I want to be.

They are my "creator" for, in truth, I came through them.
They invested all they could with tools they had back then.
They encouraged me to seek out mentors who could guide;
      this, so I'd fulfill potential – mine, deep down inside.

They made many errors in their judgment as I grew.
I know love and safety were their gifts to see me through.
They were there for me without a question or a doubt.
Now I'm here for them to see they'll never go without.

He so gently steadies her, to ease each step she takes.
Worries for, at times, her hand extended sometimes shakes.
Tucks her in and trims her nails; he listens for her call.
Watches her so carefully to catch if she should fall.
She scolds him, then thanks him for all that he means to her.
Memories – most true, some false; it seems life was a blur.
But so filled with meaning as they shared their ups and downs.
Planted seeds and watched them grow . . . their gratitude was found.
Life brought them together, so well suited – they felt 'home' . . .
As I live and breathe, I'll be sure neither is alone.
There are some days Dad and I discuss what's yet to be.

Have it figured out, but that's just intellect, you see.
My emotions cannot grasp what my head seems to know.
G-d, is this my challenge? Must my heart learn to let go?
Or, perhaps "let go" is not quite what I need to learn.
I don't really understand how Sun and Moon take turns.
Sure, embracing blessings can enrich each day we're here . . .
I can channel energy to heal pain, grief, and fear.
Guess the lesson simply put is how to honor time . . .
Heal myself mind/ body/ spirit . . . learning to say: "mine."
Make my life a blessing – YES! That's what I now must learn,
     so I can feel fulfilled, as I look back, when it's my turn.

# This Time Around

I wish I could share with you all that I hear and see.
But these sights and sounds are sadly meant for only me.

Names I utter are of people long ago, back when . . .
before the lifetime we share now – I see them all again.

Children I keep looking at have all been born before . . .
They are coming back to us; of this you can be sure.

When I call you other names, please know that they're all you.
Others who you were – so many lifetimes we've been through.

Shared forever . . . ups and downs - each time: no memory . . .
But fear not, my darling - this is how it's meant to be.

When I am no longer in the body of this life,
you will mourn the loss of all shared when I was your wife.

Please know that this life of ours: our love, this time around,
is etched in our forever – and again it will be found.

## Your thoughts

# Two Shoes

I have a name – but you call me three, as if each is a part of me.
Random switches . . . name to name, as if a childhood guessing game.
What the doctors said you'd do . . . but we hoped it would not come true.

Told us that the medication might delay this conversation.
Tough to watch you slip away from who we knew, just yesterday.

To Dad you say, "Who are you? I want my husband!" That's hard, too . . .
Seems, at times, you cannot see - then other times, you smile at me.
Seems, at times, you cannot hear, but then you greet when we come near.

"Two Shoes" – your new name for me. I wonder how this came to be?
Is the reference simply put in no relation to one's foot?
Or rather, who you choose to see, as if it's just one part of me?

When we struggled through my teens, we argued more than anything.
Once I hit age 32, our mother/daughter friendship grew.
Helped me with my marriage woes. Gave me strength and helped me grow.
Tons of milestones we came through . . . you were my rock, and I thank you.
When you look into my eyes and smile, "Two Shoes!" I realize
I'm comforted that I can see acceptance when you look at me.
Dad says, "Please, love, take these pills" and "No!" you say, and battle still –
the difficulty all uphill . . .
Turns to me and gives a glance, then I approach as happenstance
and you say, "Two-Shoes! I want YOU!"
Now it's *my* turn to do for you.

# Time is Precious (The Blanket)

This blanket is not just a blanket. It's something that keeps me in place.
This blanket feels just like a prison. It fills me with fear and disgrace.

*You're right it is not just a blanket. While true that it can keep you warm,*
*let's call this blanket our 'exercise mat' and move it to help you get strong.*

Last night I prepared all the actors, and nobody cared for the show.
Nobody came – it was such a shame. I felt so embarrassed you know.

*Please tell me about all those actors, and why you're embarrassed today.*

I just can't remember the details now. You know sometimes I get that way.

*I'm smiling at you – can you see me? I'm glad we're together right now.*

You don't understand, I hate being this way.
This cruel life has robbed me like how!

*I'm hugging you now, can you feel me? I'm here – so is Dad, by your side.*
*You don't always hear us - you're never alone.*

You DON'T understand . . . it's my PRIDE! So how many wigs do I have there?

*You have four; one gray and three brown.*

I TOLD him that but he said, "You have just one!" I told him to get out of town!
Whenever I ask him a question, he answers with lies – doesn't care.
My heart overflows with great sadness; my spirit is filled with despair.
Why doesn't he listen to questions? Why doesn't he answer with truth?

*Be real, Mom, this argument is reminiscent of all that I heard in my youth.*

And then we both break into laughter. We're blessed knowing 'now' is a gift . . .
Empowered by giving control over blankets . . . assisting through words, as we sift.
She hears & sees what seems so real. In gratitude I realize
this time with my mom is so precious - and not defined by ears or eyes.

# Her Living Legacy

Grandma loved you dearly. There was so much to see.
Didn't know all that there was before what came to be.

Grandma was so filled with love and lots of energy.
Shared it with the four of you - her living legacy.

I knew Mom as difficult. We often disagreed.
Then I had a child; our friendship grew to meet our needs.

As a grandma, she showed kindness; wanted me to see
      the loving side her motherhood did not reveal to me.
Once she was called Grandma, she embraced that role and name.
Saw her through a different lens, and things were not the same.
Her grandkids were everything – you meant the world to her.
Love she felt lit up her life . . . "old motherhood" - a blur.

Time forced her true spirit to accept and lean on me.
Life threatened her body, as it stole her dignity.
Then I met the child she was – a part I never knew.
Got to know her hopes and fears – in me, compassion grew.

I hope you can feel her spirit now that she is free.
Echoes of her wishes are so very clear to see.
Whispering: "Dear Children, though 'gone' I now live in you.
I hope all the love I feel will always see you through.
Please don't be the worst in me, just be the best in you.
This is what I hope and pray: that G-d will be with you."

# Happy Mother's Day

*Mom, it's been a while now – in fact, more than a year.*
*Seems I feel you much more deeply than when you were here.*
*Now I listen to advice you whisper to my heart.*
*When my eyes get misty – it's your hugs, though we're apart.*
*Thank you, Mom, for all the times you tried to be your best.*
*Neither you nor I passed every mother/daughter test.*
*Yes, we're both forgiven by each other – this, I know.*
*I hope you are proud of how much you have seen me grow.*
*It took motherhood for me to join the page you're on.*
*I appreciate your Spirit more since you've been gone.*
*Now that it's been almost 18 months, I clearly see*
*just how much of you still guides and lives inside of me.*
*You are with me always; here's to you this Mother's Day.*
*I know you still tuck me in – I feel you when I pray*

# Longing

Just a piece of paper - but still so hard to do.
Memories are fresh on every one I'm sorting through.

Just a piece of plastic - but your face in black and white
     tugs my heart because I know you won't come home tonight.

Just a piece of fabric and your perfume lingers still.
Empty as I hold it - how I long for you to fill:
     the fabric . . . hold the plastic . . . take the paper in your hand.
Your side of life's tapestry for YOU to understand.
Yet here I am still missing you . . . your eyes, your laugh, your hand.

# Meet Me in The Blend

Going on two years now that I seemed to leave your view.
Nights and days are difficult – the same for me and you.
I've been working hard to learn just how to hold your hand.
One day, when I master it, I'll help you understand.
Yesterday at hearts and rainbows, you smiled; I achieved
lesson number one to help you know I did not leave.

Thank you for your faith – I'm grateful that you do believe . . .
Little signals help us both as we are forced to grieve.
Lesson number two is what I mastered just last night.
As you slept you felt me without tears – it was just right.
So connected – yes, we are and, as such we depend
on truth and knowing that we're both united – without end.

When I master lesson number three, you'll feel my hug
without a tear – your heart will light up when we both think of
the memories we made when we could feel each other's touch.
Thank you for your faith in love – I miss you just as much.
When I master lesson number four there won't be fear.
I'll dissolve regret and grief – you'll be sure I'm right here.
I have many lessons still to learn – and so do you.
I now guide all loved ones with new wisdom strong and true.
Lesson number five is 'whispers' . . . gently guide with thought.
That's perhaps one of the best of all that I've been taught.
Lesson number six for me: beginning, meeting, end . . .
Comes in dreams; once mastered we meet loved ones in the blend.
Lesson number seven melts distraction – still to learn . . .
Those who live must channel peace, until it is their turn.
Though I haven't mastered six, I'll skip ahead to send
an invitation: "RSVP, 'date night' in the blend."

# My Plea to The Universe

Here I sit before you. Once again, I plead to go.
Missing my love terribly - more than my tears can show.
Hair reflects your milky way, and as I bend my head to pray . . .
Whether it's by night or day, I cringe when in my dreams you say:
*"No, not yet, it's not your time. Your tasks not yet complete."*
All I want: to reunite; yet still you just repeat:

*"No, not yet, it's not your time."*

What must I do to go?

*"Butterflies and trees will tell you.*
*When it's time, you'll know."*

I have no idea what you expect – what must I do?

*"Heal the wounds, but only those that hide inside of you.*
*You can't heal the parts that fester – broken in another.*
*Start: forgive the ignorance of your father and mother.*
*Then forgive yourself for judgment all these decades strong.*
*These become the seeds you plant to those who come along."*

I must mend the family – for I'm the reason why!

*"True, in part – but you must understand, the rest: a lie.*
*Your task now is to let go of guilt, remorse, and grief.*
*Only then will you beam forth vibrations of relief.*
*Empathy and harmony – for you to generate . . .*
*sacred keys to healing.*
*Where there's life it's not too late.*
*Joy, peace, and acceptance must be able to take hold.*
*Let them grow and find a home in you–"*

No! I'm too old!

*"Time does decorate your face with memories and grief.*
*You'll rest once you choose to trade the 'bitter' for 'relief'."*

Then five gentle butterflies all danced about my head.
I smiled once I realized all that the angel said.
We shared life – now memories . . . some painful – some divine.
Children born to us saw good and bad – some hers, some mine.
Always meant well, though as kids we had kids of our own.
Looking back sometimes I'm shocked at how well both have grown.
I do not, if truth be told, yet fully understand
how they both went on to be successful; was not by *my* hand.

They have traveled paths a plenty . . . did not come from me.
Choosing colors in their lives that my eyes could not see.

When kids outgrow parents' rules, they free themselves to grow
without the limits set by fear and guilt - new seeds they sow.
One day I will see my children own their pain and joy.
Own their choices, laughter, bliss . . . what they do and avoid.
My kids have kids of their own – I hope they can take pride
in all they choose and what they don't . . .
then, once I'm on the other side
of life's confusing tapestry, embroidered with division,
I believe I'll see it all with wisdom tinted vision.

At this time, I realize the blessing I have had.
Shared my heart – my soulmate left me with the good and bad.
Now I know what I must do to hug her once again . . .
Butterflies will all return, but welcome only when
I pass along vibrations that reveal how I bless all.

I trust my kids can and will at times stumble and fall.
Confident they both have courage fed by love, they'll mend;
but only once it's truth without distraction or pretend.

I'll now set examples from this very moment on
    to show respect, love, and acceptance, so that once I'm gone
I will carry confidence that I've provided tools
    for future generations – in accordance with *their* rules,
      to use, avoid, and contemplate . . . my task will be complete.
Inspired by the promise: once again, my love I'll meet.

*Your thoughts*

# Dear Gramma

Thank you for the love you showed when you were here with Gramps.
You two shared such magic in your eyes with every glance.
Sadly, my own Mom and Dad did not discover love,
      but having you in my youth gave me faith in God above.
Dad once said that happiness and love are just a myth.
Mom gave up on Dad – now I don't know who she is with.
I hope they found what they need and, frankly I lost track.
Sad to say, the mixed vibes aren't something I need back.

I know you'd approve of who I chose - he is to me
      the answer to my prayers and dreams. In his blue eyes I see
            pure magic – as you shared with Gramps. I feel love in his touch.
Gramps will walk me down the aisle . . . Gram, I miss you so much.

Since you've passed, you're everywhere, and on my wedding day
      you'll be more than in my heart – your presence I'll display.
I will wear your wedding dress – it's 'old' and 'borrowed', too.
In my hand, your handkerchief, your name is stitched in blue.

More than 'things' I'll keep with me the wisdom from your voice:
      "Patience, kindness, gentleness must always be the choice."
I'm so grateful for the patience you had in my youth –
Also, for your kindness and your gentle ways . . . in truth
      you have always been my teacher - helped me find my voice.
In my soul your wisdom guides through every single choice.

# Rainbows and Hearts

You come to me in rainbows and in hearts
You show me just how the connection starts.

On your plane you touch me yet anew
Reminding me again of how our love grew.

Once more you're so far ahead of me
And showing our love still yet to be.

Your messages are written in the light
And visits that are made to me at night.

All speak to my heart with this mention
"Pay heed my love, pay attention."

I will fulfill my mission dear love,
Even though I yearn to join you above.

Know that I know you are here
My wife, my sweetheart, my love, my dear.

The rest of our tale is yet to be told
To those that follow – those who are bold.

Bold enough to dare to love and embrace
To experience, to fall, to rise to the race

Of love everlasting – of love that is true
Of life beyond life, of more than we knew,

When we were parts of the rainbow
*© 2019 by Daniel Cohen*

# Today

The joy you felt this morning while the slumber filled your eyes
was me; I've mastered how to break through 'death' –
that great disguise.
The veil that keeps me from you – what we thought was just 'the end' . . .
So powerful our love – now you can feel me through the blend.

Took 3 years and 9 months, but today we felt relief.
Up to now tears wet your cheeks - for all you felt was grief.

I'm beside you every moment – through the pain and pleasure.
I will never leave you . . . and I want for you to treasure
every second of the life you're living, though I'm gone.
We dance through our spirits though from flesh I have moved on.

There will be tough days ahead with stormy, bitter weather.
We're both counting moments until we're again together.

Now your tasks (not yet complete) will take some energy.
Know for certain I am here – with you I'll always be.

# Happy Birthday Mom

*(From This Side of Life's Tapestry)*

Happy Birthday Mom. You would be 91 today.
You have been so busy - and I feel what you convey.
Lessons you paid forward when I looked into your eyes
       define me; at ***that*** time, I didn't think you were so wise.

Truth is I am who I am because of DNA . . . but also from
       your efforts – all you did and didn't say.
As I think about you it's now crystal clear to me
       all throughout my childhood you set my spirit free.

You insisted my potential was mine to fulfill.
You refused to let me worship you – and even still
       when I call on Reiki, when I need to speak to you,
         answers carry keys to inner strength to see me through.

You crossed through the tapestry 4 years ago last week.
I can feel your empathy and hugs each time we speak.

Now your caring warms me without guilt, regret, or tears . . .
Now your lessons light my path to guide me through my fears.
Now I see illusions as distractions from my goal . . .
Now I see what you saw when you looked into my soul.

I'm not falsely 'worshipping' – there is no pedestal.
I'm just sharing how I feel. Today my heart is full.
Thank you for these past four years – and how you mothered me.
Happy Birthday Mom from this side of life's tapestry.

# Connected

You're in rays of sunshine as they dance on morning dew.
You share wisdom, whispering through mountaintops in view.
Butterflies bring messages to flowers they explore.
Answers travel through the stems to earth so deep and sure.
Dawn breaks. Birds find breakfast. Crisp fresh dew drops quench their thirst.
Meadow offers magic crafted by the Universe.
That's how we're connected even though you left this earth.
You're not just a memory – because, when you gave birth,
you began the decades of mixed vibes that filled our years.
Saw me through my adolescent heartbreaks drowned in tears.
Strengthened me, determined to block passage of your fears . . .
Protected me from poison, though you didn't always steer
me in the best direction – angels know: you did you best
to help me gain the confidence years never failed to test.
You know that I feel alone. You sense my deep despair.
And when I need you most, Mom, I can feel that you're still there.

# A Promise Broken

Thank you for the gift of life – though it's hard to believe
     my tasks: now complete. Too young; thus, you're now forced to grieve.
Memories of lessons learned – of all you taught to me
     did sink in; I took them with my spirit that's now free.
Once I learn just how to bring a smile back to your face,
     I will offer laughter to you; sorrow, I'll erase.
It will take some time for me to master lessons here.
Please know I am safe; don't have concern, regret, or fear.
Dad, I'm really sorry for the sad stuff we went through.
I know there's no blame; "let go" - the first thing we must do.
Death feels like a broken promise; natural to reject
     anything that messes with the path that we expect.
Flesh does not define my spirit – now I'm free to learn
     how to comfort loved ones 'til we meet – when it's their turn.
Now I understand and soon I hope to help you see
     all the goodness you pay forward are your gifts to me.
Please live on and listen for my messages that heal.
I'll be there in butterflies and happiness you feel.
I will bring you rainbows, crickets chirping, hawks in flight.
I will bring you stars that shine as diamonds in the night.
I will be beside you every moment of each day.
I will float in hearts on walls; I'll hear you when you pray.
Know that you must live your life one moment at a time.
Take deep breaths, my father – know I'm glad that you were mine.
I know that these words can't really bring enough relief
     to the aching heart you have that overflows with grief.
Dad, know even though the path we're forced on breaks our plans:
I feel blessed for time shared; know we're both safe in God's hands.

49

Love Lost

# Anatomy of a Breakup

How can you lose her? So easy to do. Just be 'selective' with texts she sends you.

When she writes loving words, answer with: 'Great!' Promise to call and then don't - or be late.

When you are triggered by something outside, don't seek support or share – just choose to hide.

Snub her completely; hold fast to your fears. Be 'self-protective' when she pleads through tears.

Keep your eyes blank – remain passive and cold. She'll see reality; truth will unfold.

Maybe for fun you can string her along, telling her, "I know just what I did wrong!"

Then be stunned when she expects you to fix
        damage done – reach into your bag of tricks.

Act confused when she won't buy into lies.

When she sees through you, feign wounded surprise.

Stay and insist you have grown and you care. Offer your love; claim she's awfully unfair.

Tell her you cherish her then fake a smile. Maintain your 'ice-man' face as if on trial.

Be who she needs when you need her assistance –
        then drop her flat; here you must be consistent.

Be your best self when you need her to do a task that means she must prioritize you.

Have faith that she will put you before her; your needs come first – her desires: a blur.

Love motivates her; a truth, to be sure. Get what you need, then feel free to ignore.

Use her; manipulate; then walk away. Parents neglected you; make your wife pay.

It's so much easier: punish your mate for trauma your parents both forced on your plate.

Toxic vibrations all poisoned your soul. Make your wife suffer as pain takes a toll.

Here's the best part – you can blame her, not you.

Just say, "I didn't know…", when she goes through
        her agony – it is all hers, you are free!

With a clear conscience say, "It's not on me!"

Say, "She's demanding, she wants way too much. I'm just a guy – no emotional crutch.

What the heck does she insist that I say?" It may take time – but you'll chase her away.

You won't be bothered with answering texts.

You won't be stressed about what might come next.

No more concern about emails or calls. Soon you won't have her there – free from it all.

Freedom from worry – no need to explain. Life to yourself. You'll be back in the game.
So, when that woman demands that she be your world, life, and lover – your priority,
   take this advice if you want to be free.
Works like a charm. I know. It worked for me.

Now I eat pizza, and I drink my beer. Bed to myself; I can stretch - she's not here.
Yeah, it was great when she catered to me; but now I relax. Life is simple; I'm free.

I cook my meals – or I don't; it's all good. Don't have to please her or 'do what I should'.
Work on my hobbies when I am at home. Place to myself – at last I'm alone!
Did make her smile – well it wasn't that hard,
  we'd laugh together – she cherished each card
   I gave her – that's if I wrote more than my name.
Truth is, in many ways we were the same.

We loved the beach; both laughed hard when we walked.
We had fun kayaking, and when we talked.
We both played chess; she helped with my creations.
Here is the point: all of those situations
  meant that I had to put strong energy
   into growth – stunted emotionally.
I was unable to give her my best. I botched the challenge. I failed love's test.
I faked it GREAT for an hour or day. Then toxic energy came out to play.
She said: "That's not 'you' – it's just an illusion".
That pissed me off. I was filled with confusion!
Bursts of frustration - had no place to turn.
Nothing made sense – though she said, "You can learn!"
She pushed too far, so I pushed her away.
That's my life story – not much more to say.

# Healthy Love is Truth

What are you protecting? Who, where, when, or how?
You insist it's "us" but show it's not each time you bow
 to fear . . . it's clear: illusions are what you choose to protect.
Love is tossed away each time you opt to just neglect
 eye contact, truth, and sharing – you consistently defer
  to hiding, lying, cheating; healthy LOVE helps both prefer
   to open up their hearts to feel all kinds of deep emotion.
Love is strength, feeds trust, respect . . . won't entertain the notion
 that it's fine to run away – for healthy love is strong.
Two in love can lean on it through what life brings along.
When there's love, each burden's half - and pleasure multiplies.
Let's be clear, it is not love as long as there are lies.

# Rainbow's End

Not about the sun or moon or any "thing" at all.
Love is strength to lift yourself; to catch *us* when we fall.
Love is courage to dissolve distractions as they flow.
Love is joy when both of us agree to not let go.

Yet, again, you disappear as if missing in action
        every time I spot the lies you feed through your distraction.

Love is showing up no matter what if there's a frown.
Love is vowing to lift up whenever one is down.
I was hurt and you ignored – so typical of you.
Misery is what you choose – what you're devoted to.

Decades pass but time stands still, when love is in the air.
Love is taking chances – having faith that two hearts share
        with empathy, compassion, interest, caring, and concern.
Love is jumping into fire – fearing not the burn.

Love is confident and certain. Love is faith that's true.
Love is what I thought we had – I've been a fool for you.
I have done it all alone – I've waited way too long.
Wish your luck. I'll help myself. I'm able, smart and strong.
I'm no longer begging – done with trying to pretend.
You have pushed – this time too far. And this is where we end.

# Fishing for Love

When it's for love and it's honest and true, give what you can. You put him before you.
Listen for 'chimes' on the phone for his text. Make yourself ready for what might come next.
When it's for love and it's honest and true, give what you can. You put her before you.
Listen for 'chimes' on the phone for her text. Answer completely and offer what's next.

When it's for love, you're alert and aware, showing you're interested; showing you care.
When it's for love you respond right on time. If you are late, don't distract – it's no crime.
Own it and step up; look into her eyes. Heart on your sleeve – don't need a disguise.

When it's for love you don't throw in a line then turn your back, walk away - THAT is a crime.
Motivate, innovate, always be there. Earn trust with empathy, presence, and care.
Love isn't misery, traps, or a noose, or 'talking your way out', excuse to excuse.

Love gives you strength to hold out your hand.
Love is a journey – in flight, and to stand
together as one; to bring comfort – share grief.
A blessing and generous; love's not a thief.
If you don't feel that your love is returned,
time to move on with the lessons you've learned.

## Your thoughts

# Awakening

Thought it was okay – one time it was. I thought we fit.
One day I said, "Run with me" but you preferred to sit.
Didn't understand and prayed each night so I could know:
"What's so wrong with me?" The message came: "It's time to grow."

Answers made no sense, then in my dreams I bled and cried.
Morning came, then images . . . with both eyes open wide
        pictures rushed into my mind – there was no place to hide.

Feelings once in shadows danced behind my lids closed tight.
There was no escape. They tortured me all day and night.
Answering my question: "First I sat, then ran . . . but why?"
Rainbows dressed in silence spelled the words: "It's time to fly."

No! Can't. Won't. Don't want to. It's familiar here, though wrong.
Then the message: "Find your courage. Fly, your wings are strong!
Sit, stand, run: no longer right – it's time to touch the sky.
Stop the struggle. Painful truth: it's time to say 'good-bye'."

Understood the message. Courage grew before too long.
Stabs of pain; excruciating - anything but strong.
Didn't want to hurt you. Staying here keeps hurting me.
How can we resolve this need to set our spirits free?

Your words: "Sit down. Stay for me. Just let this feeling pass."
30 years through broken trust, like splintered fragile glass,
        pushed me to this moment – that is why I had to stand.
You don't bleed, but I do . . . and my blood is on your hand.

You still fail to notice. If you truly cared for me,
        you'd find the way to rebuild trust - or set my spirit free.
"Predictable" is NOT 'trust' – and your isolating wall
        exhausts me; I can't break through. When I try, I fail. I crawl.

Knees scraped; broken glass . . . you have no empathy at all.
Bolted shut those windows as you sit behind your door.
You shout: "I'm here waiting." But what am *I* waiting for?
Will you find your courage? Is your personality
          something I pretended? Truth is sharp in clarity.
Built my world around you – and yet you still choose to be
          self-protective, self-absorbed. No room for 'us' or 'we'.

*Your thoughts*

# The Search for Meaning in Our Union

Through the years we've loved as one, embracing our shared life.
Marriage, started out: white water as husband and wife.
Each a wounded toddler playing out the unresolved . . .
Painful childhood memories we both sought to dissolve.
Guided by the Universe we found the way to earn
       each other's trust – through growing pains . . . so much still left to learn.
Was ours a 'soul contract' or could we be guided by
       an angel who blessed us to help each other scale the sky?

Words and understanding are so meaningful to me.
You're the artist – we're both blessed with creativity.
Decades in this world together, trust and love were found.
We felt safe when our eyes met – as if this time around
       was just 'continuation' of a life we shared before.
It is now three decades with so much yet to explore.

Arguments, resistance and refusal to let go . . .
Obstacles distract us from ways we still need to grow.

Suddenly it's clear that when I share, I feel ignored.
Empty eyes – you're absent . . . love should never be a chore.
Though I trust you with my life, my heart begs you to learn
       how to share as we once did . . . my trust you must re-earn.
When we met, we felt complete. We had sparks in our eyes.
Now I feel you hide from me – your inner voice now lies.
Our love: like an onion, tears with layers as we peel;
       we re-frame to take new steps, then levels soon reveal
         answers and more questions as together we invest
           energy in love to pass the Universe's test.

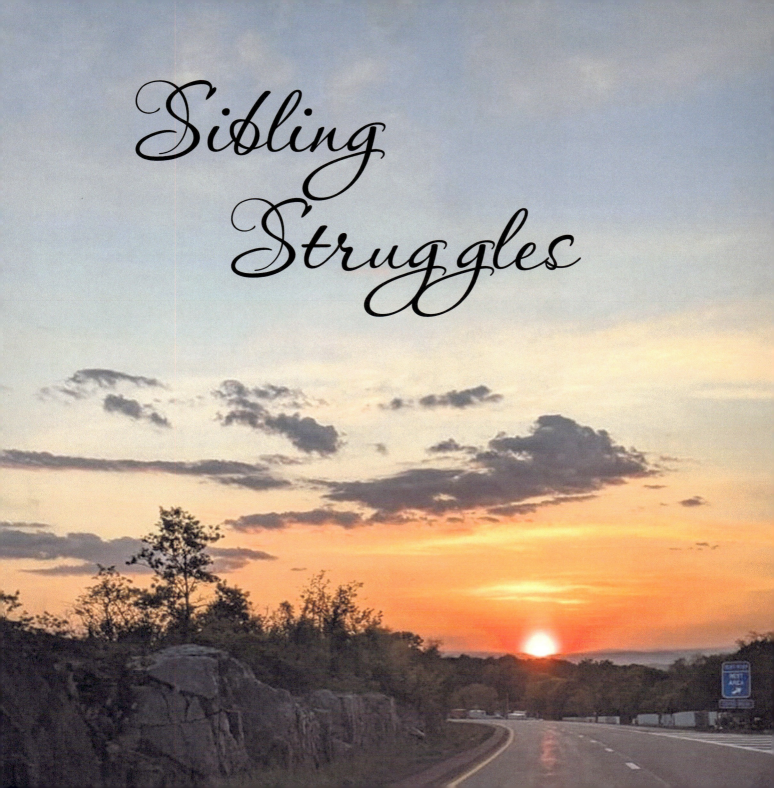

# Believe the Lie

My mistake: I rocked her boat. She says I'm always wrong.
Dad said: "You must cater to your wife." Am I that strong?

Now I find I must distract from what, in truth, I'd see.
I've become a master of illusion to feel free.

What I value more than you: to maintain status quo;
and my reputation – thus, of you I must let go.
I'm a married man now; I have children of my own.
Siblinghood is in the past – our sharing, I've outgrown.
I know that we promised we would never turn our back
on each other; now we are like Mom and Uncle Jack.
Promises we made to always be there for each other:
I must break; my wife hates you, so, I can't be your brother.
Don't care what I put you through – can't help it if you cry.
I choose to ignore and hide; I must believe the lie.

# Keeping the Light On

Never dreamed I'd see this day when from my heart I'd ever say:
"Thank you for the years of lies;" through tears I've shed, I realize:
       pain forced my inner strength to rise.
Couldn't grasp the choice you said your wife forced you to make.
Siblinghood competes with marriage? Oh, give me a break!
First you chose to shut me out, you said "to honor her."
Suddenly, you now blame *me* – for you, 'truth' is a blur.
You confessed, "'She told the kids you're evil'. That was wrong!
       I will not permit it!"
At that time, you were so strong.
You buy into falsehoods and the venom that you spew
       doesn't say what I'm about – but it reflects on you.
Still, I'm here with open heart until the day I die.
I will keep our childhood promise. You believe your lie.

# Estranged

Years of pushing me away with venom that you spew,
      clarified the painful path you chose to drag us through.
Once a gentle spirit, you now mock respect . . . choose fear;
      finger on the jugular of those that you hold dear.
Since you trashed my family, among a few conclusions:
      there's no trust 'til you stop manufacturing delusions.
You fuel toxic energy. You're covered in a cloud.
You believe false memories and you say them out loud.
Through the darkness that encircles you, by your own choice,
      I can't help but wonder if you hear your inner voice.
Do you ever listen to the truth within your soul?
Seems as if you're in reverse: your diamond heart now coal.
Has your spirit song become one note – no melody?
You forced me to lock my door – though you still have a key.
You craft lies; ignore the facts; I'm trying to let go . . .
Hoping you awaken from this nightmare; let me know.

# Mixed Vibrations

I don't understand what's going on inside of you!
Acting like I've done you wrong with things I put you through.
Sure, I didn't tell you when I turned my phone to 'fax'.
Didn't let you know I was in town a few months back.

Yes, I did inform you that I cannot say your name
    if my wife is home – cause when I do, she goes insane.
I know I decided not to show on New Year's Eve.
That's because my wife refused – she flat out wouldn't leave.
You don't know what I go through at home – for decades now.
I gave up so much I loved – was tough, but I learned how.
I know we made promises that we would never be
    like siblings filled with hate; since then, things changed – at least, for me.
No choice but to blame you as if you forced an assault.
My truth is too painful; won't accept my choice; my fault.
You are way too wordy; I can't answer every text.
Emails make my eyes bleed – I cringe wondering "what's next?"
Face it: you're high maintenance. I've got no time for you.
I'm a busy man with more important things to do.
You were always driving Mom so crazy way back then.
Have not changed a bit; you still can't filter or pretend.

Every time I speak, you want to understand each word!
Why you need 'to clarify' is NUTS! You are absurd!
I don't have the energy to help you understand.
You expect I'll show up just because it's what we planned.
Look, I can't be bothered – I just do what I can do . . .
I'm your brother, as such, I am always here for you.

# Despair – The Great Pretender

Aching anguish . . . painful grief.
All I dream of is relief.
I resent the goal: "the race . . ."
     to earn my final resting place
        for if I fail, I'll bring disgrace
           upon myself; to those who see . . .
             to all upon my family tree.
Birds fly high. They sail and soar.
Their freedom dance I can't ignore.
The clouds above trees – they explore.

Oh, if I could be a bird!
Alas, the thought is so absurd!
Envy as I watch the geese . . .
     they honk; formation, their release.
Jealous of the morning sparrow,
     speed and grace – flight straight and narrow.

Torturous anxiety.
Deep breaths; air won't set me free.

At once I feel my time grows near. What will come next? I shake with fear.
For me this life has ne'er been fun. The dewdrops glisten in the sun.
The rabbits and the frogs all hop as if they never want to stop.
The turtles bask in summer rays; self-contentment as they gaze.
They never seem to be impressed by hummingbirds – with wings so dressed
     in rainbows, as they hover by.
The turtle's shell, though dull and dry – upon it, turtle can rely.
As I recall my springtime dance, when flowers filled air with romance . . .
     a memory of summer breeze; of nests built high on strong proud trees.
Then thoughts of colors as they change; when dreams were mine to rearrange.

Now winter's here. It feels so strange.
I think of all the moments spent . . . of time so wasted in lament.
I think now of this final breeze. Filled by a chill – emotions freeze.
A sudden 'snap' . . . what do I feel? Just like a bird – my dreams are real.
I taste the breeze without remorse. You know I am a leaf, of course.

So, next time you observe a dance of brown leaves: know each took the chance
      to flutter like a butterfly; to glide as birds soar through the sky . . .
          . . . to sail as long as time would grant; to live a dream before they plant
          the stories of all that they'd learned.
All wisdom for the hungry worms
      who thus consume, and pass along through birds who share them in their songs.
Alas, my life was not a waste.
Through soil I'll offer all a taste
      so that perhaps another may
          appreciate each bright, new day.

*Your thoughts*

# Voices Within

While in the chrysalis, as wings take their form, Butterfly listens to Universal Energy's gentle explanation to all in The Meadow.

"I offer you 'worry' as a tool. Use it to pay attention to your inner wisdom and whispering angels. Tune into your *iwwa* whenever you feel concern."

Recalling the 'concerns' of caterpillars, always fearful of birds, wasps, stink bugs and so many things in The Meadow, Butterfly wonders, "But what if I can't hear my *iwwa*?"

Butterfly's thoughts are answered, as Universal Energy hears all. "Dear Butterfly, that question is asked by every generation of all life in The Meadow. Namaste on your thoughtful query.

"But how do you hear my thoughts?" asks Butterfly from deep inside the chrysalis.

"Yours is but just a single voice in a magnificent chorus of all in your generation. You might not hear others as they ask, but take comfort in knowing that your thoughts are magnified by all who wonder from within their chrysalis. I am always listening."

A deep sigh of comfort is taken by all who feel the answer. Universal Energy continues, "During this part of your journey, you hear my voice in answer to your concerns. Once you emerge, my voice will be channeled through your *iwwa*. You hear me now, before rebirth. Soon, you will arrive to balance The Meadow, guided by your *iwwa*. Listen well to remain true to the spirit that lives within you."

"Will my *iwwa* always be there to ease concern and worry?" ask all butterflies separately, yet in precise unison, each from within their chrysalis.

"Yes," reassures Universal Energy.

At this point, a snake slithers, tapping interruption into the soil with its forked tongue. The formality of Universal Energy is an excruciating irritation to Snake, who takes great pleasure in offering distraction. "This is untrue," Snake hisses. "I know of many who have no *iwwa*. They are filled with anxiety and nervous tension. They lose their way through distraction and fear."

A chill bites the air. Butterflies from within their chrysalises shiver simultaneously at the interruption.

"Deep breath," whispers Universal Energy.

All from within their chrysalis listen and follow Universal Energy's directions.

"Very good. You are all doing well," says Universal Energy.

"Is what Snake tapped true?" ask all unformed butterflies with one voice.

In answer, Universal Energy sends dancing butterflies and bees to hover and share their experience. Gentle Breeze helps deliver messages that butterflies and bees sing to the next generation.

The messages are clear. "Danger rankles in partial truths. Snake warns about runaway anxiety, nervous tension, distraction, and fear; however, these illusions are a result of denial of one's *iwwa* rather than lack of *iwwa* itself. All have *iwwa*. The ability to tune into *iwwa* often takes a lifetime to master. *Iwwa* helps us fulfill our unique destiny to balance The Meadow."

"But how do we know if we're hearing truth? How do we know what to believe? Snake tries to trick us with a partial truth. How do we know our place?" ask unformed butterflies from their chrysalises. Anxiety and tension fill the walls of each chrysalis.

Universal Energy permits butterflies and bees to dance the answer. Their dance reveals: *"Joy. When you are doing what you are intended to do to balance The Meadow, you feel joy, followed by inner peace, satisfaction, and balance within your own spirit. Joy is what guides you."*

Universal Energy asks, "Did you feel that dance?"

Snake's forked tongue again hisses interruption into the soil, "Lies. They don't mention shame. Ask about when joy is followed by guilt and shame!"

In response to Snake's chill, a kaleidoscope of butterflies lifts from meadow flowers; a concerned swarm of bees joins them. A gentle, warm breeze hushes The Meadow. Universal Energy whispers to butterflies and bees through fragrances of milkweed, honeysuckle, Echinacea, and roses. All flowers join to share the message of wisdom. Butterflies and bees breathe deeply, then gently rest back where they were before Snake's interruption.

"What was that?" ask butterflies from inside their chrysalises.

Universal Energy explains, "Fragrance carries my messages. You experienced the dances in response, but failed to hear my message. Listen again." With that, Universal Energy inspires a repeat of the message through the flowers: *"When true to your spirit, you balance The Meadow. In time you learn the difference between 'repose from distraction' and 'joy from fulfilling your potential'. Your purpose is to balance The Meadow with gifts you have yet to discover."*

In response to that repeat message, the kaleidoscope of butterflies and swarm of bees once again dance - but only the second part of their prior dance.

"But that is only half the dance," observe the unhatched butterflies.

"Excellent observation," states Universal Energy. "The first part - choreographed by Alarm, was the dance of worry. The second part, choreographed by Awakening, was the dance of joy. Without Awakening, there is an opportunity for shame and guilt to distract Creatures of The Meadow from fulfilling their destiny. Your observation of the dance choreographed by Awakening is one you must remember and embrace."

All from within their chrysalises respond in unison, "We heard and felt that dance of joy."

Universal Energy replies, "Excellent. That is exactly what your *iwwa* will sound and feel like. You are ready my dear butterflies. Prepare to embark upon the next phase of your continuing journey."

At once, wings clap from inside their chrysalises, then spread in appreciation of the message about joy. In strength, all tear through their darkened, thinning shells. Butterflies free themselves to dry their wings, preparing to join in a dance of their own. The first dance choreographed by Freedom. Each butterfly takes a unique path.

A brand-new adventure. So many paths through the wide-open sky. Each butterfly experiences The Meadow uniquely, at first. With patience, butterflies learn how to tune into *iwwa*, and, with experience, master worry as well as frustration. Discovering how illusive Awakening can be, once a butterfly befriends that choreographer, mastery of the dance of joy soon follows. From that point forward, destiny welcomes each butterfly . . . and all rejoice in taking their proper place in balance with fellow Creatures of The Meadow.

*Your thoughts*

# Earthworm and Caterpillar

Rainbows connect tales of the soil to what become legends of the stars. True love is the key – permitting only those who experience it to drink wisdom. Most can observe beauty. Very few are able to grasp the essence of each message.

When centered peace and joy free spirits to recognize intricate patterns crafted by *iwwa*, the Universe opens to embrace all – even those still on this side of life's tapestry. Such was the discovery of Earthworm, after his struggle – and failure, to keep up with Caterpillar.

This is the tale of how Butterfly learned that, though her whispers were unable to be heard by her dearly adored Earthworm, the love they shared was a magical and eternal portal through which communication would be able to take place. Not only did it offer memories of all that united them during exciting escapades, before Caterpillar's ascent up the bark of a tree, but it also lit the way – through rainbows – to show how stars store the tales. The heavens blended time – past, present, and future, comforting both, until reunited and able to add new tales of separate adventures; new tales to the soil, and legends to the stars.

Baffled by the disappearance of Caterpillar, as well as by the vision of a beautiful butterfly – who fluttered with a language so foreign, Earthworm was overcome by fear, loneliness, and frustration. These strangers accompanied him as he crept back down the four inches he was able to climb. Earthworm dug more deeply into the soil than ever before. It seemed a lifetime ago when Caterpillar was with Earthworm. At that time, Earthworm had no desire to dig as deeply as he was able. He preferred to stay near Caterpillar – who was unable to accompany him to the world beneath the soil.

Suddenly, Earthworm began to hear sounds that never before caught his attention. "Were they always there?" he wondered. Then, an answer from another Earthworm who seemed very much older.

"They've always been here. You just never knew how to listen. You must have lost someone you dearly loved," shared the Elder Earthworm.

"Yes. I have," shared Earthworm. Then he addressed the Elder, "But how did you hear my thoughts?"

"I have always heard your thoughts. It is you who are finally able to hear mine. This is growth. You should be proud."

"I'm too sad to be proud of anything. I'm too angry, confused, frustrated and upset to think right now," exclaimed Earthworm.

"Yes. I know," said the Elder.

"What do you know?"

"I know about loss, grief, and living on," said the Elder.

A brief silence was interrupted by another sound. It didn't come from the Elder or from Earthworm. It was as strange as it was familiar. "What is that?" asked Earthworm.

"Those are your memories. Snapshots of time shared with Caterpillar."

"I don't understand," said Earthworm, on the verge of tears.

"Each memory shared is preserved as a tale within the soil. All done is recorded and told by trees during the months of slumber, when all rooted life above the soil drink from history made on this side of the tapestry. The trees are most gifted, as they translate stories that arrive through rainbows from the stars. History then repeats itself, in one form or another."

"That makes no sense whatsoever," declared Earthworm. Then, added, "I'm sorry. I shouldn't have been rude. You are trying to teach me."

The Elder reassured, "Anger is easier to experience than is grief. Your self-reflection is admirable. You are growing very fast," said the Elder.

"What does that mean? I'm no larger than I was a moment ago."

"Internal growth enriches the spirit. Soon you will be able to drink wisdom from all the tales – those of times shared with Caterpillar, and even tales of the soil absorbed from so many others who lived lives upon which you've never before focused."

"So, you're saying that my life with Caterpillar was somehow recorded by the soil?"

"Yes."

"Why did I never hear the tales when I dug before?" asked Earthworm.

"You never went deeply enough, and you didn't know how to listen. The journey is not only physical - it is spiritual as well. You were simply unready until this moment in time."

Earthworm had much to think about. So many new ideas to consider and process. This took a great many days. After realizing how far into the earth he was able to go, he realized that before, though he believed he dug deeply, he barely scratched the surface. Now there was an entire world he was ready to explore, and as he did so, something amazing happened.

"Caterpillar? Is that you?" asked Earthworm.

No answer.

Earthworm searched for the Elder to ask about the unusual experience of feeling as if Caterpillar was near him.

"You have found the connection. Excellent," declared the Elder who seemed unreasonably delighted with Earthworm's confusion.

"I don't understand your pleasure at my frustration!" declared Earthworm.

"There you go again," chucked the Elder, lightheartedly. "Permitting anger to distract from your sadness; confusion and frustration to cloud your heart. You can do better. Try again," encouraged the Elder.

"I think you are insensitive, unkind, and unfeeling," stated Earthworm, bluntly.

"Is this about me? Is that why you sought me out?"

"No. I wanted to ask your advice and for your wisdom, but I find you to be cold hearted and uncaring," stated Earthworm.

"And how, might I ask, have you arrived at this conclusion?"

"I came to ask for your help and you mock me," stated Earthworm.

"How exactly do I mock you?"

Earthworm thought about it and realized that all the Elder did was reflect joy and respect for what Earthworm shared. But Earthworm, upset and confused, permitted frustration about the initial situation to distract him from hearing truth.

"As I think about it now, perhaps I was defensive for no good reason," admitted Earthworm.

"You are marvelous," declared the Elder. "Now to the point that brought you to me today," encouraged the Elder.

"I thought you could hear my thoughts?"

"I can. It is not for me to hear as much as it is for you to hear yourself. As time will teach you, there are answers which embed themselves in statements and questions. That is to say, the effort and thought you experience while preparing to share out loud may assist in your finding the truth within your own self," said the Elder.

"You speak in riddles and that is irritating," stated the Earthworm.

"Deep breath."

Both Earthworm and the Elder took a deep breath together. The Elder broke the silence with his observation. "You heard Caterpillar?"

"Well, it's more like I *felt* Caterpillar," corrected Earthworm.

"And how did the experience feel?" asked the Elder.

"Sad. She was sad, and I was sad for her," shared Earthworm.

The Elder pondered before speaking slowly. "You have an extraordinary gift Earthworm. You are able to feel Caterpillar so soon – even during your grief. Remarkable. This is so very rare. Your love must have been unspeakably powerful."

"Can you say that in a way I can actually understand?" asked Earthworm.

"What you are now ready to learn is how to communicate with Caterpillar. You are able to realize that she was as confused as were you upon her emergence from her chrysalis."

"You are using words I don't understand."

"You are an earthworm. You fell in love with a caterpillar. You are not the same."

Earthworm became angry with the Elder. "You don't know a thing about Caterpillar! You sound just like my family and friends. I don't need this from you!"

"Is this anger about me or about your feelings about your family and friends?"

"They all rejected our union."

"Ah. This is not about what I am speaking. You are, in fact, different from Caterpillar. She could not dig into the earth and you could not spin silk or form a chrysalis. These facts are not any creature's 'fault'. They are simply the way of The Meadow."

"You sound ignorant! We WERE the same. We loved sharing everything! We shared our entire life. We WERE the same," insisted Earthworm.

"In many ways, you were indeed the same. You were both the same in that you shared the gifts of truth and trust. This grew into love. You were able to look past the external – into each other's soul. That is indeed precious and exactly what nourishes your connection right now."

"I'm still not getting your point here."

"Let's return to your decision to seek me out. You felt Caterpillar, right?"

"Right."

"And you felt that she was sad. Right?"

"Right."

"What I'm telling you now is, just as you felt confusion and grief when she emerged as a butterfly –"

"Wait, WHAT?" interrupted Earthworm. "She emerged as a WHAT?" he asked with growing anxiety.

"A butterfly. You didn't realize that?" asked the Elder.

"Are you trying to make me feel stupid?" asked Earthworm.

The Elder pondered a moment, realizing that assumptions needed to be tempered. Earthworm was, indeed, still in the early stages of grief.

"I am so sorry," said the Elder. "I need to explain a few things to you. And no, I don't think you are stupid and you shouldn't either. This was my fault entirely."

Earthworm remained silent.

The Elder began, "Just as you struggled to climb the tree – against everything you felt was natural for you to do – am I right?"

"Yes. Go on," encouraged Earthworm.

"Okay. You climbed the tree because you wanted to keep Caterpillar safe – but what you didn't know was that caterpillars have a desire to climb flowers or trees – far from their host plants, just as earthworms need to dig into the soil. You are each correct – for your own kind. Keep listening. Stay patient with me, okay?"

"Yes. I'm listening."

"All right then. Caterpillar needed to climb the tree, spin the silk, form a chrysalis, and then emerge as a butterfly. I know it sounds unbelievable but it's true. She entered The Meadow as a caterpillar, destined to become a butterfly. When she finally emerged, she was devastated, as were you. Each butterfly has brief and scattered memories of life before the chrysalis, but love is something they can't leave behind. She emerged and felt a strong longing for you, her dear Earthworm."

Earthworm remained silent. This was a lot of information to absorb.

"So, you see, Earthworm – your dear Caterpillar never left you. She emerged to embark upon the new phase of her continuing journey. And what you felt from her was not sadness but longing – as she remembered you and your shared love."

"But how can I communicate with her? You said there were tales? How do I get them into the soil?"

"This discussion has already become part of the tales, and seeds of milkweed are drinking them as we share. Your Butterfly will soon lay eggs on the leaves, and when those eggs hatch, her future generations will eat the leaves which carry the stories."

"So, then she won't ever get my messages?" lamented Earthworm.

"We are but dust in the circle of life, Earthworm. It isn't about each of us as individuals, but about how we prepare for the generations that follow – so that they can protect the earth and channel positive energy and joy. The love, goodness, and devotion you put into the soil through honest sharing and trust are all helping to balance the earth. This is your continuing journey to help the earth balance the Universe.

But you're sensing something about butterfly - as she is now, suggests she is also sensing something about you. She will seek wisdom from her mentors along her continuing journey. So, dear Earthworm, this leads us all to admire the rainbows as those carry dreams, magic, legends of the stars, and tales of the soil. Every Creature of The Meadow intuitively understands the promise of the rainbow."

Earthworm felt abandoned by the Elder as his quest was to reunite with Caterpillar. Crestfallen, he ventured back up to the surface, shedding silent tears of heartbreak. Thunderstorms threatened with bolts of lightning over meadows in the distance. He was grateful to have made his way safely to the surface before the earth flooded him out.

Hours passed. The storm tore through his meadow, leaving behind a crisp, clear double rainbow. Earthworm marveled at the brilliance of the colors. The first time he ever looked up above the grass was to try to follow Caterpillar. Now he was looking up alone, feeling forlorn, until suddenly, a vision he had never before encountered. It was the butterfly that emerged from Caterpillar's chrysalis. Earthworm rushed to the tree where they departed, and Butterfly lit upon a blade of grass to be close to her dearly adored Earthworm. A hummingbird darted over them hovering just long enough to offer them their own rainbow through its wings.

# Confessions of a Swallowtail

Leaves were sweet. We all agreed. The time was right. "Climb down!"
The stalk was long. Now we were free to meet the earth . . . the ground.
Cool and welcoming it was. Our bellies: satisfied.
Leaves provided strength for us. Now was the time to slide.

Dirt felt soft, so I ignored the feet that I could have.
I preferred to hug the earth; this made my siblings sad.
None of them could understand why I chose what I did.
I could not explain myself. To self-protect: I hid.
I rejected energy they forced – how I resisted!
They continued in their chants; in one voice they insisted:
     "Our destiny: to taste all flowers from above!
         We are tasked to make lines in the Sky – the breeze to love."

Each of many siblings tried their best to thus advise.
Such an irritation – soon I came to just despise.
     "Come with us to choose our spot – we'll spin silk strong and sure;
         suspended in our chrysalis we'll share dreams to explore."

After Sun shared with bright Moon more days than I could count,
     I met worms and heard their stories – soon I could recount
         stories 'as if' I lived them – as if I took their place.
I imagined I had pain that they tried to erase.

Each explained the horrors of the birds they had to fear.
Even while safe underground, the sharp beaks they could hear.
In my heart I felt their anguish, as each took a turn,
     sharing of the trauma; all at once I came to learn:
I was sent to help them heal; thought I must feel the same.
Had to share their trauma – though I had no birds to blame.

I did not come from the ground. I hatched. Ate leaves all green – not brown.

And yet I felt to share their grief was how I could bring them relief.
To that end: I hid my feet.

I was able to assist in ways they said: "You can't."
I heard stories told by bees, mosquitoes, ticks, and ants.
They spoke as if wise, "There's no way *you* can help a worm!
How to heal from pecking birds is something you can't learn."

Well, I proved The Meadow wrong and I helped far and wide
       all the worms who came to me – they found their strength to slide
             where they wanted; when they wanted; I taught them to hear
                   flapping wings from far above – in time, they had no fear.
No surprising beaks could reach them. They learned to dig deep.
All my students learned so well; the lessons they will keep . . .
Limited was I by tales I heard before I hatched.
Following my destiny – sometimes hurts to look back.
Not because of what I did – I healed trauma and pain
       in so many worms, although in truth "worm's" not my name.

I pretended to be one of them so they could hear.
I believed I had to be a worm – I had my fear
       that if they saw my feet they'd just ignore; thought I was wise.
I feared if they knew my truth, then I would be despised.
Well, I proved it to myself – I healed them all the same.
Now it's time to join my siblings – time to heal *my* pain.

Climbed far from my host plant. So surprised was I to see
       all my siblings fluttering around – they came for me.
They were told by Owl that my journey was unique.
I became a chrysalis. At once I could not speak.

Once enveloped, couldn't see – but so much I could hear.
Tales so crisp, and through the stalk the worms were very clear.
I was shocked to learn they didn't care that I had feet.
Valuing my wisdom, they were grateful just to meet

a creature of The Meadow who they knew one day would fly.
Each one valued me for ME! Why did I have to lie?

Worms embraced my spirit, knowing I could mend and heal.
I had no idea . . . embarrassed now, I tried to steal
      identity – was not my own. This shame stirred deep in me.
All at once just silence . . . then explosive energy.
Tearing through the chrysalis with wings that set me free.
Fluttering I joined my siblings in our family tree.

*Your thoughts*

# Moving On

Crawling through the morning . . . spinning silk by afternoon.
Twilight greets the evening. Dawn says 'farewell' to the Moon.
Rays of Summer Sun all beckon; growing restlessness.
Nature calls, insisting you tear through your chrysalis.

Stretching wings, you realize: no longer legs to crawl.
Wondering when you will glide . . . you try - again, you fall.
Moth befriends you gently, and it teaches you to flutter.
Both together, you take flight - then suddenly you shudder.

Once you see reflected in the clear green pond below,
yours a dance of grace with Mentor Moth - and you both know:
Morning light puts moth to sleep - your day has just begun.
Moth must work by moonlight; to sow seeds, you need the Sun.

Time repeats: the moth must rest; your task: to flutter on.
The Meadow, daytime mentorship; you sleep from dusk to dawn.
When Sun's rays invite the Moon and that favor's returned,
Dusk and Dawn provide the moments; you share what you've learned.

Moth and you delight in dance as Sun and Moon share Sky.
They instruct The Meadow - teaching Moth and Butterfly
how to share and balance . . . catching breezes, passing tests.
Moments are invested - each works while the other rests.

# Destiny

I'm afraid to taste," said Honey Bee to Butterfly.

*"I don't understand – you are a Bee. Please tell me why?"*

"Flowers are so pretty but it's quite enough for me
      to buzz around – don't care to touch; contented just to see."

*"I must sip each flower and then flutter high through trees.*
*I enjoy the misty air and gliding on each breeze.*
*I assist, by tasting – I help flowers multiply.*
*Honey Bee, I'm still confused. You don't taste? Tell me why."*

"If I taste the flowers then one day they aren't there,
      I'm afraid I'll miss them . . . so I never ever dare."

Butterfly was sad to see that fear distracted Honey Bee.

*"Honey Bee, we have important jobs that we must do.*
*One day flowers free their seeds – that fact is strong and true.*
*Did you ever stop to think you pollinate them as you drink?"*

Honey Bee thought all about what Butterfly had said.
Fear was blocking joy - and that was all inside his head.
Honey Bee began to ponder and, as he was thinking
      Butterfly screamed with delight, *"That's GREAT! I see you're drinking!"*
Honey Bee then realized the moment that they shared
      would last forever; Honey Bee felt blessed that his friend cared.
Butterfly helped Honey Bee explore each opportunity.
Honey made with fellow bees enriched the logs of fallen trees.
Springtime flowers then became a very different form and name
      as petals fell and joined the earth, preparing soil for their rebirth.
Future seeds were sown in place. Honey Bee slowed down in pace.

Butterfly did slow down, too. Together they shared all they knew,
and every moment they lived through.

Honey Bee felt gratitude for Butterfly that day.
Inner dialogue repeated all she had to say.
Thoughts about his path and fears – how she taught him to see.
Helped him cry, then dried his tears. She set his spirit free.
When they met, could not reflect; awakened, he felt strong.
All at once, while drinking his wings buzzed his spirit song.

Recognizing all the effort shared by Butterfly,
Honey Bee embraced the truth: his 'job' more than just 'fly'.

Thus, his understanding of The Meadow and his place
nourished self-esteem; no longer lost – all fears erased.

"Bursting now with memories of honeysuckle, birds, and trees,
dear Butterfly, each flit and dart brought me such joy – you filled my heart.
To you I feel deep gratitude. You helped me change my attitude."
As Butterfly thanked Honey Bee, they both fulfilled their destiny.

*Your thoughts*

# Beneath the Surface

May not seem like much to you -
     my task is Soil to slip through.
Far beneath what Eagle sees,
     without me there might be no trees.
You're as proud as you can be
     with beauty in your wings – so free
        to flutter over far and wide
          with dips and turns – each breeze you glide.
Meadows all yours to explore,
     not quite as the eagles soar . . .
Yet your value is unmatched,
     as eggs you lay – like birds, they hatch.
Balance is what we're here for . . . my value easy to ignore.
Meadow knows all that I do.
There is a place for me and you.

In Meadow's time we rest and toil.
My humble task: maintain the soil.

# Can't Make a Flower Grow by Pulling on Its Stem

Power lies in silence when the lesson to convey
       is meant to help another grow - for words get in the way.

Flowers blossom fed by roots –
       not from a stem that's pulled.
Wisdom speaks through silence; all too often we are fooled
       to force a resolution so an argument can end.
This just feeds distraction used to con, deflect, pretend.

Wisdom is a spirit truth – it's not a tool to lend.
Effort to force others is a way to lose a friend.

Those who pull at stems just strangle – blossoms cannot grow.
Fact: that chokes and blocks all that the spirit needs to know.

Patience, faith, and silence are what true growth really needs.
After flowers blossom, they will often spread their seeds.

Don't attempt to pull at stems or force slumber to wake.
Focusing on stems – though it's a chance you want to take,
       results in pure disaster as a strangled stem will break.

# Said Rosebush to the Oak

So sad that I had to die to set your spirit free.
Now my shadow's gone; you have great strength; now we both see.
Stand up tall my child - as you are meant to be a tree.

I was your protection once you rolled down from that hill.
Promised Earth and Meadow I'd protect you up until
      the time was right, but I could not be certain – not at all
            exactly when your strength was there to see the Oak leaves fall.
Thoughts: "It will upset you"- tried to shield you from the pain.
Now that I see through the soil, the truth I can reclaim.
Seasons change and it was not a favor done for you
      to block the dances of the leaves, Sun's rays, or morning dew.
I've joined all that came before and now your time is here
      to fulfill your destiny; deep roots; dissolve all fear.
Your place is to be Great Oak, in Meadow – strong and sure.
View the valley from your mountain – never to ignore
      breezes filled with messages, and lessons yet to learn.
Then you channel them to earth, and when it is your turn
      set your acorns free, and then you'll wish them to fulfill
            Universal destiny – following their will.
Let go of illusions; let them find truth – taste each lie.
Have faith acorns grow from storms, and learn when parched & dry.
Understand our journey through vast time has just begun.
Roots unite us through the soil – in truth, we're part of one.

# Stink Bug and The Moon

The night was pretty quiet, filled with house lights soft and low.
The Sun was setting gently. The evening sky a glow.
The kids were tucked in sweetly. My pillow so divine.
The day was filled with fear and toil. A deep breath on my mind.
All muscles: weak and weary. Organic raised beds done.
A few weeks 'til the plants arrive. My work has just begun.
This year my crop is not from seeds, but each day I well know
the ones I plant in life indeed I'll nourish so they grow.
My children watch my every move, and how I handle fear.
So closely they observe my smiles and every single tear.
The world is now in crisis from what's called COVID-19.
But it did not begin here - I know YOU know what I mean.

Suddenly awakening awareness – global, true.
Today a virus – but be clear, there more we need to do.
Earth is filled with goodness, but as clouds get in the way
warms rays blocked; we just see clouds, though Sun shines every day.

Head upon my pillow as I drift to welcome sleep.
A large sound past my head reminds: a promise I must keep.
Reluctantly with slippers on I find the cup and card
to catch that little stink bug that makes slumber oh so hard.

I searched beneath the lampshade - and there it was for me
to safely catch so I could set the little stink bug free.
Didn't want to wake the kids by opening the door,
but had no choice - this stink bug had the evening to explore.

Once outside I shook the cup - the gift he gave to me:
a view of Hunter's Moon. So glorious a sight to see!

If I had been fast asleep, I'd miss that evening hug.
The moon was standing watch. I am so grateful to Stink Bug.

# Dissolve the Excuse (COVID-19)

Brush up on reframing – an important thing to do.
Invest in all that lifts you up – a skill to get you through
the scariest and darkest days, when loneliness can try
to block the healing energy you carry deep inside.

Since this virus separates . . . embrace what unifies:
Zooming, Skyping, making calls, are platforms that defy
distraction from communicating with the friends we love.
Where there's true desire, you and I can rise above.

Stuck at home? Play music. Organize your closets, too.
Bake, read, write, dance – do all that you had no time to do
before coronavirus redefined your daily plan.
Truth is: now's the time to play the cards held in your hand.

What was on your list of things you just could not get to
because of all the outside chores you 'just had to get through'?
Now's the time to paint, sew, draw . . . or find a new skill to explore.
Imagination is your clue . . . as always, steps are up to you.

# Sacred Path

When a child is told, "Be quiet. Don't share if you're 'sad'!"
Seeds are planted. Anger grows . . . becoming toxic 'mad'.
Feelings of abandonment begin to churn inside.
Self-protective lessons: "Do **not** 'feel' – just learn to hide."
Anger turns to guilt because, of course, to *feel* is wrong.
Self-protective lessons now: "Be distant to be strong."

If per chance adulthood introduces love or joy,
wild confusion – "Love feels GOOD!"
The reflex: to destroy.
Anything that might bring pleasure: break, because you're sure
distance equals strength; thus, feeling 'love' you must ignore.
Self-destructive inner dialogue will not permit
experiencing happiness – your spirit takes a hit.
Are you wounded toddler, or the parent in this tale?
Do you have a loved one who is burdened – young or frail?

Time, as long as there is life and 'will', is on your side.
Make the choice to heal and mend – to redefine inside
the meaning of your life; the sacred journey you now choose.
If your choice thwarts love and kindness, everyone must lose.

# You Have Arrived

*Once you can . . .*

. . . cut out those who slap you when you're generous and kind.

. . . step away from those who twist the truth; seek those who find
      beauty in the world – they manufacture happiness.

. . . know what you deserve; expect it; settle for no less.

. . . empower those around you just by shining your warm light.

. . . help lift tortured people frightened by each starless night.

. . . retain your hard-earned dignity, while others beat you down.

. . . stay open; don't play 'victim'; sidestep bowing to false crowns.

. . . offer from your heart without the trap to 'over-give'.

. . . honor your own spirit; know your truth; live and let live.

. . . settle down – don't settle 'for' – win battles for your soul.

. . . balance intellect, love, caring – know 'hate' takes a toll.

. . . give your best and do what channels pure sweet energy.

. . . make a goal to give your all – be ALL you're meant to be.

. . . feed another's confidence until they take that role.

. . . manufacture healing when you find another stole –
      or tried to steal your courage, leaving you without a tool
         to rebuild what you had – wake up: don't think you were a fool.

. . . learn your lessons; pay them forward - never with contempt.

. . . know the Universe is paid one day: none are exempt.

. . . feel true pleasure when you give; pay honest, close attention.

. . . actively share kindness without constant need to mention.

. . . keep in mind the crop you sow from all that you have planted
      are for all who pitch in – not those who take you for granted.

. . . trust and earn another's trust – when broken strive to mend.

. . . honestly feed truth to spirit – don't try to pretend.

. . . be a caring person for the world, and take great pride
      in winning all the soulful battles raging on inside.

# *Open Heart*

Easy to open all windows when there is a promise of sunshine all day.
What of erroneous forecasts that fail to report a big storm on the way?

After decades marked by rainclouds barely lined by Sun,
    tough to open windows – if you do . . . prepared to run.
Clearing countertops protecting what might get destroyed
    if you dare to take the chance – defensiveness employed.
"Clear skies promised; sunny day ahead" . . . but can you trust
    the words you want to hear? The answer: "NO" and yet, you must.
Believing "clear skies / sunshine" is a risky, foolish bet;
    self-protective vows include: prepare to get quite wet.
Hesitation. You resist as there's no trust until
    sunshine streams through windows closed, protecting every sill.
Though consistent sunshine – you fear shun time will appear . . .
    clouds of disappointment linger . . . PTSD's here.

How much will you risk for love you once thought you could share?
How courageous must you be . . . when sun and clouds are always there?

Years are filled with forecasts. One day windows open wide.
Courage overtakes the fear. Confusion set aside.
Standing ready, you observe the new forecast just might
    provide a restful day of comfort – no bad dreams at night.

Window sills of open hearts stay dry and safe, and then . . .
    you embrace the trust well earned. Your paths as one, again.

# My Spirit to Yours

Your spirit is valuable, unique, & *exactly* as it was designed to be.

You are *powerful.*
Your journey is *sacred.*
Your decisions are *yours.*

You are *responsible.*
All steps you take & avoid: *your choice.*
Your heart *knows* the truth – *always.*

If it 'feels wrong' it is because it *is* wrong.
If it 'feels right' it is because it *is* right.

Love is truth, and the goal of life.
Positive energy is the pure channel of love.

Clouds are there to strengthen you.
See beyond the clouds to find your rainbow.

# Evil Twin

Every person on this planet has an evil twin.
Healthy spirits know it and define the source within.
Raised without support and love portends a joyless fate.
Grow away from negativity before too late.
If it goes 'unnoticed' you risk torture to your soul.
If you spot it early on – the truth will soon unfold.
'Evil twin' inspires mischief; limit testing, too.
Healthy boundaries must be set to help young spirits through.
Parenting that's caring keeps you safe until you grow;
        first you recognize your inner light, then seeds you sow
            to reveal next steps: to channel healing energy.
Self-define then choose the path to be all you can be.
If your spirit falls through cracks in Toyland – not your fault.
Recognize the source of the unfortunate assault.
Evil twin will twist reality until you do.
Battle and true victory – accomplished by too few.
If you see your evil twin, if toe-to-toe you meet,
        to feed your spirit: cut the ties; sift truth from all deceit.
Certainty can point the light dissolving shadows cast;
        thus, to see the object as it is; lies of the past
            no longer have a hold on you; begin your task at will.
The future can be bright but there's no happiness until
        you recognize the spark of the divine shines strong within.
All yours once victorious against your evil twin.

# Aunt Tilly & Uncle Bob

Aunt 'T' so opinionated – thinks she knows what's best.
Sometimes seems well meaning – other times she seems possessed.
Uncle Bob can't be pinned down – ignores, gaslights, deflects.
Wanting to be catered to; prefers 'fear' to 'respect'.

Every family has an Aunt T and/or Uncle Bob.
Sometimes twisted forms of each pretending it's your job
to satisfy – though, truth be told, their toxic energy
sucks the air out of the room
so healthy people flee.
Set safe boundaries; that's the cure . . . and here's Step #1:
know yourself, be your best friend - once you catch on, it's fun.
Step 2: find your inner peace – your personality.
It's revealed with cleansing breaths to set your spirit free.
How do you define your life? What's "comfort", "joy", and "peace"?
Understand your value; blissful vibes; exhale; release.

Once you find your balance, you're embarking on Step 3.
Another cleansing breath to channel healing energy.

# Things Should Be Like This

When we lose a loved one, what matters is we miss
      fulfillment of our expectation: "Things should be like this . . ."
A sister with no brother or a wife without her spouse . . .
An orphan who has parents - sometimes life is just about
      connections we make with our maker - guiding angels, too;
         ones that whisper softly with supportive flags and clues.

Death has many faces, so does life - both so complex.
Life and death feed gratitude; both make us ask: "What's next?"
Gratitude is fed when expectation is fulfilled.
Burying our disappointment feeds grief which is fueled
      by blocking of the energy that's meant to heal and give
         abundant joy in sharing heartfelt moments while we live.
When love's unconditional, that is the way to measure
      how much distance you should keep; in truth: embrace that treasure.
Villain/ victim/ savior scripts are not for healthy hearts.
Fueling toxic energy – they split loved ones apart.
Walls: unnatural boundaries when in weakness we define
      a caring family member as 'the stranger' any time.
Siblings forced to call each other "villain" is a clue.
Spouses don't share values? That's a separation, too.
Children, when they self-discover ethics that collide
      with those taught by their parents:
         there's more death though they're alive.
Many ways to lose a loved one. Bottom line: we miss
      fulfillment of the expectation: "Things should be like this."

# Wishing to Undo

Mom I've done a lot of stuff I wish I could undo.
Humiliation is the price I've paid – I can't face you.

*Honey, we've all made mistakes – no matter what you've done,*
*you are welcome home; no need to talk, avoid, or run.*
*When and if you're ready, please know I'm right here for you.*
*I know your true spirit and, whatever you've been through,*
*I hope you can understand you're always in my heart . . .*
*Love you as I always have, though years we've been apart.*

I can't hold my head up high. I can't come home – not now.

*"Can't" is a distraction from your growth – and you know how.*
*Step one: find your truth; face where you were and where you are.*
*Step two: where you want to be; these first steps take you far.*

Mom, don't say, "I told you so" I hate it when you do.
If you promise, I'll consider coming home to you.

# *Truth to Spirit*

Two things often rented, for they can't be bought or sold:
    one is heart-felt happiness; the other is the soul.
Number one, when 'just for show' means 'heart-felt' is a lie.
Number two can shred the spirit, mended only if you try
    honestly to match all actions with words and intent . . .
Truth is clear and G-d sees when the devil pays its rent.
If the happiness is true, it channels energy:
    joyful glances cast by eyes for everyone to see.
If the soul is filled with gratitude, it can't be bought,
Heart-filled joy and love are vibes that can't be faked or taught.

*Your thoughts*

# Alien Dictionary

Body language of Ms. Kitten baffles Pup when it is smitten.
Cat tail twitch means, "Go away" - but puppy tail wag means, "Let's play!"
How can two relax in fun when Pup says, "Stay" but Cat hears, "RUN!"?

Puppies soon learn they need more than cardboard boxes to explore.
Dogs need love, companionship . . . communication, too.
Dogs enjoy relaxing by a campfire all night through.
Dogs thrive on heartfelt attention; loyal to the end.
Dogs show love and empathy. On Dog, Cat can depend.

Cat is independent and, at times, could not care less
        about Dog's expectations; thus, in truth all must confess:
When Dog calls Ms. Cat, Dog can't be certain Cat will show.
When Ms. Cat calls Dog – well, Dog's response Cat surely knows.

Sad, but true, Dog can expect that Cat will often spew neglect.
Cat won't share; walk by Dog's side . . . from warm embraces - Cat will hide.
Cat so easily distracted – shadows, bugs, and rays of light
        all become a friend or foe against which Cat must fight.
Dog prefers to snuggle up with Cat, but Cat can't rest.
Cat is self-indulgent – often fails the snuggle test.

Trust is difficult to build unless both can define
        the meaning of each twitch and wag, and venture to refine
                communication, signals or, at least to understand.
Without clear understanding, two can't share or make a plan.

If you are the Dog and your life partner is the Cat,
        trust becomes tough to invest – just Dogs are built like that.
It is in Dog's nature to be loyal and protect . . .
This is something healthy partners equally project.
If love shared is mutual – then Cat must self-expect

much more than its nature; cuddle, share, and show respect.
Dog who holds back tail wags – that loving energy,
        soon feels deep frustration, as that feeds anxiety.
Dog must be permitted to be all that it can be.
That's the only way to set Dog's spirit truly free.
Dogs in a relationship all want and need to share . . .
Sadly, all too often, cats force dogs into despair.
Magical when Dog and Cat relax and play together.
Rare, but very possible – with love, each storm they weather.
Cats can master cuddling. To trust? That too, they learn.
It takes dedication, time, and patience with each turn.

Only when there's loyalty – a crucial guiding key
        may two embrace, as soulmates, throughout their eternity.

If your spirit is of Dog, though actions mimic Cat,
        that's a path to starve your soul – rethink, and then turn back.
When two hearts share gratitude, dark threads enforce their bond.
Trust can quench a spirit parched by lies told from beyond.
Time reveals all obstacles designed for us to see.
Universe weaves every thread of life's great tapestry.

# Finally

You awaken my heart in ways he could not.
You're always on time – no excuse: "I forgot".
You honor my tears; clear up my confusion . . .
For decades he said my love's just an intrusion.
Now I feel valuable, precious, alive . . .
I'm my best self since together we strive
        to earn sacred trust and feed all that is good.
I've waited for decades, and cried over "should" . . .
You are here now – and together we live.
Don't suck my joy . . . you add to it; you give.
Finally, in your arms I can feel "home'.
Soulmates forever – we're never alone.

# Generating Magic

When you fuel your spirit with pure generosity,
        positive vibrations are so clear for all to see.
Generate this essence and you channel golden light
        which emanates from glances cast; each sense you thus ignite.
Inner truth beams brilliantly, dissolving all pretense;
        nourishing emotion - your world suddenly makes sense.
Colors dance much brighter; sweet aroma fills your soul.
Every sound in harmony . . . so wisdom can unfold.
You taste strands of Universe, and when you meet another
        who can generate this energy – there is no other
        you can see yourself with; both are bound through time as one.
Thus, the great adventure we call life has just begun.

# The Journey Shared as One

Parents stole your childhood; you treat me as 'Mom' you hate.

Decades since we took our vows . . . I fear growth is too late.

Neither of us understood . . . we've now awakened to
>    the fact that neither one deserved what you have put us through.

Ready for a man – a spouse, a husband to fulfill
>    the promises we made when we began to climb life's hill.

Dreamed of life together. Trust, love, walking hand-in-hand.

If you want "rekindled love" – you'll have to take a stand.

Our love must be mutual with effort strong and true.

Not forced or one-sided; it's what both must want to do.

Happiness is nurtured; joy must be a common goal.

Time defines priorities. Your dead eyes took a toll.

Love is effort towards the other's comfort, can't you see?

Caring must be honest. It brings pure sweet harmony
>    to the rhythm of shared life. You don't do that for me.

You preferred, for all these years, to fight, flee, and destroy -
>    always choosing misery above laughter and joy.

Love is feeling safe: of spirit, body, soul, and mind.

Love first sparks, then trust is earned. There's no need to "remind."

Love is not defensive. It is natural. Heart wide open.

Love is a solution – not 'attack' until one's broken.

Love is feeling 'home' in every aspect of your life.

Love is sacred; counting blessings as husband and wife.

Tinder sparks a flame - then both, together, gather wood.

Resting by the embers not because you think you 'should'.

Once you learn to gather, feed, share, nourish, and be true,
>    I will see the soulmate who so long ago I knew.

# Quest

One Who Sees will guide you to the path that is your name.
Soul contract; acceptance to dissolve fear, guilt, and shame.
Answering the question: "why" invites your sacred quest.
Your task: to embark; embrace yourself to pass life's test.

This side of the tapestry: a pattern of loose threads.
Tangled are the offerings: joy, hope, love, fear, and dread.
Childhood, if threatening: survival tools you craft.
Leave those tools in Toyland; truth to self means "don't look back."
True adulthood brings joy when of old tools you lose track.

Once across the threshold, seek out bright threads - soft and fine.
Self-reflect and you'll discover sparks of the Divine.
Each a sacred path. Free will. Find mentors who are wise.
Learn well to choose joy above gloom cleverly disguised.
Nourish your mind/ body/ spirit balance – feed your soul.
Now a diamond in the rough. We all begin as coal.
Arrival: when you focus on the spark that lives in you.
Through love touch eternity – a gift to precious few.

Posters

To earn
trust
make a promise & keep it.
Works EVERY time!

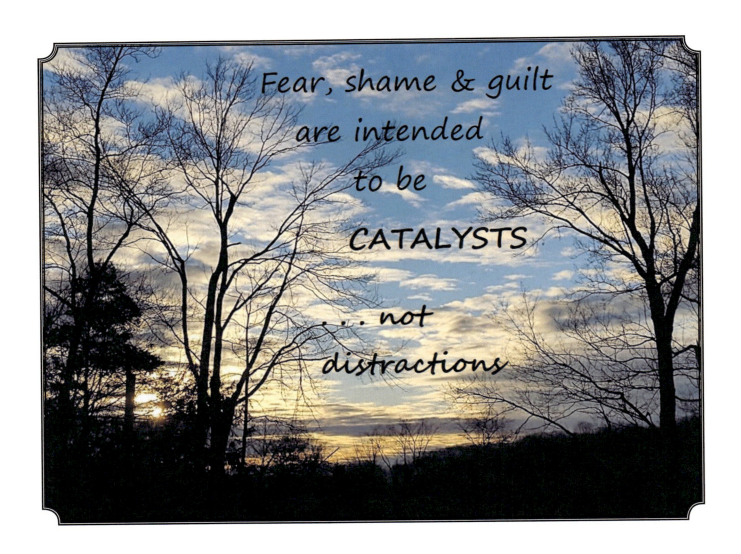

Fear, shame & guilt

are intended

to be

CATALYSTS

. . . not

distractions

Today is the first day of the REST of your life.
Embrace it with gratitude, positive energy &
a heartfelt desire to spread healing vibrations.

Universe's Secretary 2020

Some of the most healing paths
are paved by those
recovering from
the deepest pain.

Healthy parenting

focuses on helping children . . .

embrace their talents & gifts

tame their distractions

accept parts of themselves that make them proud

feel SEEN when they succeed

feel SUPPORTED when they fail

Universe's Secretary 2020

. . . and NEVER controls through fear,
shame, or guilt.

When 'home' is a place we escape TO rather than FROM,

. . . we have ARRIVED.

Universe's Secretary 2020

The most DECORATIVE threads along life's tapestry are created by

some of the most DIFFICULT moments we're forced to endure.

Embrace the beauty.

Cherish the moments.

Express GRATITUDE for the opportunity to

experience each new day.

This is YOUR life. YOUR sacred journey.

ALL steps taken and avoided: YOUR choice.

Universe's Secretary 2020

# Monarch and Sparrow

Said Monarch to Sparrow: "Let's race through the Sky."
"But I can't reach those treetops! I'm not a butterfly."
Monarch then encouraged, "If you would drop that leaf,
You could fly as high as I . . . "
Bird sighed without relief.
"Alas dear Monarch, this is where our paths
must sadly part."
"But Sparrow - there's much left to share,
this path is just the start."
Sparrow thought he wanted to -
but could not drop the leaf.
Fear could not be washed away
by silent tears of grief.
Sparrow made his choice - and Monarch
sadly flew away . . .
Praying Sparrow had the strength
to free himself one day.

Although my childhood was
STOLEN from me . . .

adulthood offers the opportunity
for ME to offer MYSELF the

caring, support, & understanding
I deserve, so that I can honestly
open my heart to trust & love.

Success isn't about floating without ripples . . .

. . . it's defined by how you handle the waves.

Universe's Secretary 2020

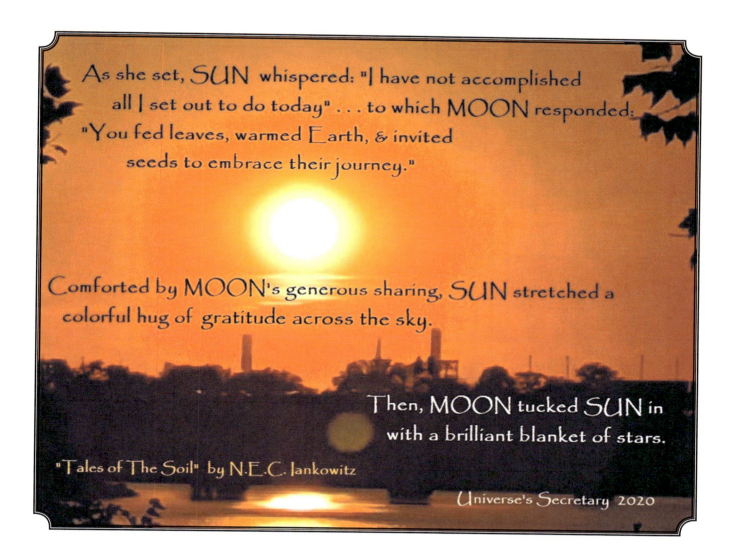

As she set, SUN whispered: "I have not accomplished all I set out to do today" . . . to which MOON responded: "You fed leaves, warmed Earth, & invited seeds to embrace their journey."

Comforted by MOON's generous sharing, SUN stretched a colorful hug of gratitude across the sky.

Then, MOON tucked SUN in with a brilliant blanket of stars.

"Tales of The Soil" by N.E.C. Jankowitz

Universe's Secretary 2020

# An Honest SMILE ...

When the heart sings, the spirit can fly.

Head in the clouds & energy high.

Goodness & gratitude – laughter & grace

All clearly seen by the look on your face.

Never be fooled by the mouth – any size

True feelings beam forth by the look in the eyes.

## . . . the eyes have it.

Universe's Secretary 2020

Vibrations created by moments shared
resonate within hearts & minds
of all who surround us.

Travel with care.

Universe's Secretary 2020

# I Believe

I believe Mom hears the music even though
we can't.
I believe she hears the voices as they sing
and chant.
I know that it's hard for you when her mind
slips and flies.
Dad, I see the sadness when I look into your eyes.
I know that you're doing everything in every way.
I know that the love you share is more than
words convey.

There's much I don't know, and then there are
things I believe…

One thing that I'm certain of is

true love never leaves.

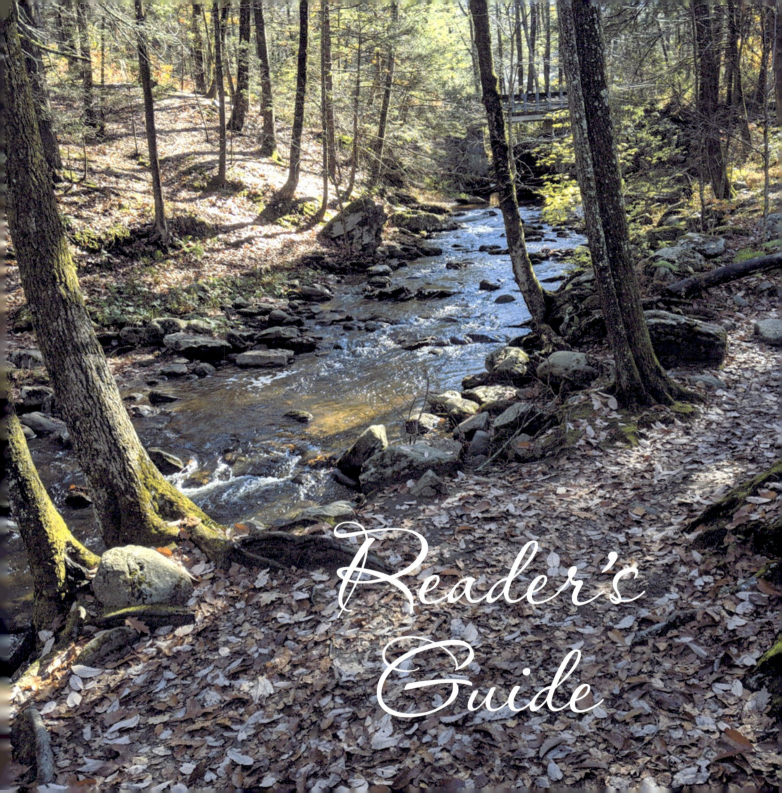

Reader's Guide

# Significant Others –Relationship Building

New Love / Second Chance / Moving On / Destiny
Evil Twin / The Journey Shared as One / Sacred Path
Anatomy of a Breakup / Fishing for Love
The Search for Meaning in Our Union / Rainbow's End
Open Heart / Alien Dictionary

# Reflection – Siblings –Complex Relationships

Battle for Your Soul / Acceptance / I Am Enough
The Bitter Taste of Distraction / Evil Twin
Believe the Lie / Keeping the Light On
Things Should Be Like This / Voices Within / Mixed Vibrations
Earthworm & Caterpillar / Confessions of a Swallowtail
Moving On / Destiny / Beneath the Surface
Can't Make a Flower Grow by Pulling on Its Stem
Alien Dictionary

# Gratitude

Stink Bug & The Moon / Dissolve the Excuse
Truth to Spirit / On Love
51 Years in Love / Finally
Generating Magic

# Personal Validation

When / Sacred Path / Aunt Tilly & Uncle Bob / Healthy Love is Truth
Despair – The Great Pretender / Truth to Spirit
Voices Within / Beneath the Surface / Things Should Be Like This

# Coping with Feelings Surrounding Aging Loved Ones

Time is Precious / The Visits Are Just Right
This Time Around / Two Shoes / Journey

# Raising Children

Strength to Let Go / Leaving Toyland Behind
Said Rosebush to the Oak
Sacred Path / Growing Pains
A Mother's Wish for Her Daughter

# Mothers and Daughters

Happy Mother's Day Mom
A Mother's Wish for Her Daughter
Said Rosebush to the Oak
Connected

# Grief and Loss

Connected / Her Living Legacy
Happy Mother's Day / Longing
Meet Me in The Blend / My Plea to The Universe
Earthworm and Caterpillar / Dear Gramma
Rainbows and Hearts / Today
Happy Birthday Mom

Printed in the United States
by Baker & Taylor Publisher Services